ETIQUETTE GUIDE TO

JAPAN

Know the rules that make the difference!

Updated and expanded edition

BOYÉ LAFAYETTE DE MENTE

TUTTLE PUBLISHING
Tokyo • Rutland, Vermont • Singapore

Published by Tuttle Publishing, an imprint of Periplus Editions (HK) Ltd., with editorial offices at 364 Innovation Drive, North Clarendon, Vermont 05759 U.S.A.

Library of Congress Cataloging-in-Publication Data
De Mente, Boye.
  Etiquette guide to Japan : know the rules that make the difference / Boyé Lafayette De Mente. — Rev. ed.
    p. cm.
  Previously published: 1990.   Includes index.
  ISBN 978-4-8053-0961-2 (pbk. : alk. paper)
  1. Etiquette—Japan. I. Title.
  BJ2007.J33D4 2009
  395.052—dc22   2008031783

Distributed by:

North America, Latin America & Europe
Tuttle Publishing
364 Innovation Drive
North Clarendon, VT 05759-9436 U.S.A.
Tel: 1 (802) 773-8930
Fax: 1 (802) 773-6993
info@tuttlepublishing.com
www.tuttlepublishing.com

Asia Pacific
Berkeley Books Pte. Ltd.
61 Tai Seng Avenue #02-12
Singapore 534167
Tel: (65) 6280-1330
Fax: (65) 6280-6290
inquiries@periplus.com.sg
www.periplus.com

Japan
Tuttle Publishing
Yaekari Building, 3rd Floor
5-4-12 Osaki
Shinagawa-ku
Tokyo 141 0032
Tel: (81) 3 5437-0171
Fax: (81) 3 5437-0755
tuttle-sales@gol.com

First edition
12 11 10 09 08   10 9 8 7 6 5 4 3 2 1

Printed in the United States of America

TUTTLE PUBLISHING® is a registered trademark of Tuttle Publishing, a division of Periplus Editions (HK) Ltd.

Contents

Notes on the Japanese Language

Much of the writing that you see in Japan will consist of the language's famous ideographic characters or *kanji* (kahn-jee), as they are called in Japanese. But virtually all of the bus, subway, train, hotel, restaurant, and shop signs and names that you encounter will also be written in the familiar Roman letters used by the English language. These Romanized words make the Japanese language surprisingly easy for Westerners to pronounce.

Japanese is based on five vowels and a number of consonants that are combined to create an alphabet of syllables that never change. The result is that there are no "weird" or unexpected spellings or pronunciations of Japanese words, unlike in English and many other languages.

Once you learn how to pronounce the vowels and the vowel-consonant combinations, you know how to pronounce every word in the Japanese language. The five Japanese vowels are represented by the Roman letters *A, I, U, E,* and *O*. They are pronounced as follows:

A	*ah*
I	*ee*
U	*uu* as in *rue*
E	*eh*
O	*oh*

These vowels are "syllables" in themselves and are key elements in the vowel-consonant combinations that make up the rest of the Japanese alphabet. The following charts include all of the syllables in the Japanese language, along with their English phonetic equivalents. Just pronounce the phonetics in standard English and the sounds will come out "in Japanese."

Primary Syllables

KA	KI	KU	KE	KO
kah	kee	kuu	kay	koe

SA	SHI	SU	SE	SO
sah	she	sue	say	so

TA	CHI	TSU	TE	TO
tah	chee	t'sue	tay	toe

NA	NI	NU	NE	NO
nah	nee	nuu	nay	no

HA	HI	HU	HE	HO
hah	hee	who	hay	hoe

MA	MI	MU	ME	MO
mah	me	moo	may	moe

YA	I	YU	E	YO
yah	ee	yuu	eh	yoe

RA	RI	RU	RE	RO
rah	ree	rue	ray	roe

(In Japanese, the letter R sounds a bit like the English letter L and often requires a slight trilling sound. You should also roll the letter R a bit when saying Japanese words.)

GA	GI	GU	GE	GO
gah	ghee	goo	gay	go

ZA	ZI	ZU	ZE	ZO
zah	jee	zoo	zay	zoe

DA	JI	ZU	DE	DO
dah	jee	zoo	day	doe

(Note that ZI *and* JI *sound virtually the same.)*

BA	BI	BU	BE	BO
bah	bee	boo	bay	boe

PA	PI	PU	PE	PO
pah	pee	puu	pay	poe

Combined Syllables

The following syllables are combinations of some of the ones appearing above. Two syllables are combined into one simply by merging them, and they are pronounced as "one" syllable, not two. *Biyu* (spelled *byu* in its combined form), for example, should be run together and sound like the *Beau* in *Beulah.*

RYA	RYU	RYO
re-yah	re-yuu	re-yoe

MYA	MYU	MYO
me-yah	me-yuu	me-yoe

NYA	NYU	NYO
ne-yah	ne-yuu	ne-yoe

HYA	HYU	HYO
he-yah	he-yuu	he-yoe

CHA	CHU	CHO
chah	chuu	choe
SHA	SHU	SHO
shah	shuu	show
KYA	KYU	KYO
q'yah	que	q'yoe
PYA	PYU	PYO
p'yah	p'yuu	p'yoe
BYA	BYU	BYO
b'yah	b'yuu	b'yoe
JA	JU	JO
jah	juu	joe
GYA	GYU	GYO
g'yah	g'yuu	g'yoe

I suggest that you practice pronouncing these syllables for several minutes until you are able to say them smoothly and without hesitation. In no time, you will be able to recognize individual syllables in the Japanese words you see and hear. The word *arigato* ("thank you"), for example, is made up of four syllables: *a-ri-ga-to* (ah-ree-gah-toe). Don't forget to trill the *ri* syllable a bit, as if it were Spanish. (In fact, most of the primary syllables outlined above are pronounced almost exactly the way they would be in Spanish.)

The letters *H* and *G* are always pronounced hard, as in *ho* and *go*. There are no true *L* or *V* sounds in Japanese, so they do not appear in the list of syllables. Because these sounds are so unfamiliar, Japanese people attempting to pronounce

English words that include them often say *R* instead of *L* and *B* instead of *V*.

Long vowels in Japanese syllables are pronounced twice as long as regular vowels and are indicated by a straight line, or macron, placed above them: ā, ī ū, ē, and ō.

Most syllables in Japanese are distinctly pronounced. At times, however, the *I* and *U* vowel sounds are weak, and the syllable is not clearly pronounced. Thus, *desu*—the verb "to be"—is pronounced *dess* and *yoroshiku* becomes *yoh-rohshh-kuu*.

English speakers traveling in Japan should also be aware that more than 20,000 English words have been integrated into the Japanese language. Rendered into Japanese syllables, they are now a fundamental part of daily speech. Virtually every Japanese conversation is peppered with these adopted words, making the study and use of the Japanese language as a whole that much easier once you get used to the system.

Of course, a Japanized English word may become meaningless to foreign ears if it is used out of context. *Bread*, for example, is pronounced *buredo* (boo-ray-doe); *milk* is pronounced *miruku* (me-rue-koo).

Again, the secret to using these pronunciation guidelines to communicate in Japanese is to pronounce the English phonetics for each word and sentence as standard English, practicing each sentence until it comes out in a smooth flow.

Preface

Etiquette as Morality

Although often overshadowed by a modern facade, long-standing traditional aspects of Japan's culture still influence the country and almost everyone in it. Concrete evidence of this traditional culture can be seen everywhere—in the ancient arts and crafts that are still important parts of everyday life, in the many shrines and temples that dot the nation, and in the modern comeback of traditional fashions such as kimono and yukata robes.

To many Western visitors, however, the most obvious example of this traditional culture's strength is the unique etiquette of the Japanese. Like many nations, Japan has experienced vast political, social, and economic change over the past century. But enough of Japan's traditional etiquette remains to set the Japanese apart socially and psychologically, and to make success in socializing and doing business with them a special challenge for Westerners.

The Japanese were certainly not the first people to create a social system based on a highly stylized form of behavior, but there have been few if any societies that carried the stylization as far as the Japanese, or made adherence to social norms such an integral part of popular culture.

For generations, the ethical and moral standards of the Japanese were measured by their knowledge of and adherence to minutely detailed etiquette. There was a prescribed form and order for virtually every action, from routine daily tasks to special occasions. Failure to follow these established forms of behavior was regarded as a transgression against the family, the community, and even the nation. In fact, one of the key elements in the Japanese social system was subsumed in the term *messhi-hoko* (may-she hoe-koe), or "self-sacrifice," which required individuals to sacrifice their personal ambitions—and often their personalities as well—for the benefit of whatever group they belonged to. The code of social conduct became so formal, so detailed, and so important that proper behavior became the paramount morality of the land, regularly taking precedence over human feelings and ethical considerations. Yet it was combined with a reverence for nature and an acute awareness of the sensual and spiritual side of life that tempered some of its harsher realities.

Despite the inroads that have been made in Japan by Westernization and modernization since the end of the country's feudal era in the 1860s, this traditional etiquette is alive and well and is tangible and visible for all to see. Even in cosmopolitan Tokyo and other Japanese cities the evidence of age-old forms of behavior is readily obvious. From the ritual of bowing to the use of special language meant to convey respect, today's etiquette can be a glimpse into Japan's distant past.

Tourists and businesspeople do not need to be overly concerned about knowing and following Japanese etiquette because the Japanese are exceptionally tolerant of visitors, whom they regard as guests, and are especially helpful in coaching visitors in all the intricacies of their traditional behavior—from meeting and greeting people, to seating considerations and dining, entertaining, and interacting with others in business and social situations.

But even a cursory knowledge of Japanese etiquette can help you avoid serious social transgressions and interact more successfully with the Japanese. It is polite, considerate, and wise to know as much as possible about Japanese etiquette and to follow it with as much skill as possible, because doing things "the right way" is the only way you can enjoy the full benefit of the unique Japanese experience.

Since Japanese etiquette is a product of the country's culture and history, learning about it and interacting with the Japanese "inside" their etiquette gives you an insight into their character and personality—which is the most valuable thing you can get from a visit to a new country. Dining the Japanese way, to provide one significant example, means "becoming Japanese" in a cultural sense. By knowing and following the traditional Japanese way of dining your experience is immeasurably deepened and becomes *real*—not just something you saw in a movie or read about in a book.

For the discerning foreign visitor, just a few days in Japan can be an extraordinary aesthetic and cultural experience. If you look closely, the whole country is a virtual museum of modern and traditional images that imbue daily life with an emotional, intellectual, and spiritual link to the past.

In fact, Western visitors to Japan who take the time to experience the aspects of ancient Japanese culture that still exist today in traditional restaurants, inns, shrines, temples, and gardens, as well as at ceremonial events such as tea ceremonies and weddings, are often so impressed with their experiences that they incorporate some of the elements of Japan's traditional culture into their own lifestyles when they return home.

Visitors who go to Japan and deliberately seek to experience elements of the traditional culture are enriched beyond words.

Boyé Lafayette De Mente
Atami, Japan

1

Origins of
Japanese Etiquette

The impetus for the development of Japan's etiquette-oriented culture no doubt came from the native religion Shinto, which translates as "Way of the Gods" and is based on maintaining harmonious relationships between mankind, nature, and the cosmos.

Shinto is essentially a type of nature worship in which all things, including rivers, rocks, and trees, are considered to have spirits to whom a degree of reverence is due—philosophical and spiritual beliefs shared by the Hopi, Navajo, and other native American tribes.

The primary focus of Japanese worship was the pantheon of Shinto gods believed to control all the forces of nature as well as the welfare of the people, including the success of crops and human fertility.

Believing that their world was inhabited by innumerable spirits and gods, the Japanese developed a respectful attitude toward the seen as well as the unseen. This attitude was to shape their character from the beginning of their history and set the stage for the emergence of one of the world's most mannered societies.

According to the creation myth of Japan, Izanagi (Ee-zah-nah-ghee) and Izanami (Ee-zah-nah-me), a god and goddess, gave birth to the Japanese islands. They were so enchanted with the beauty of their handiwork that they descended from the heavens to live on the islands. The story goes on to say that the Japanese themselves were the descendants of lesser gods who also settled on the island chain.

The lineage of Japan's earliest leaders, who combined the functions of high priest and sovereign, was traced directly to the divine ancestors in whose name they ruled. Thus, from the dawn of its history, Japanese society was structured according to religious tenets that required a very circumspect behavior and numerous formal ceremonies.

Another factor that was to play a crucial role in the development of etiquette in Japan was the sweeping importation beginning in the mid-sixth century of Korean and Chinese fashions, philosophies, and social customs.

Japan borrowed extensively from China in particular. By that time, China was already over three thousand years old and had a highly refined and stylized culture based on a concept familiar to the Japanese—a godlike emperor ruling over vassals and slaves and supported by a hierarchy of powerful underlings whose stations also entitled them to reverential treatment.

China's contributions to Japanese civilization included its writing system, styles and techniques of art and architecture, technology, medicine, and religious, philosophical, and legal systems. The heart of the Chinese system of etiquette was the culture of the Imperial Court in the Chinese capital, and this became the model for the Japanese.

2

The Role of Harmony

According to legend, Japan's first imperial government dated from around 600 BC. It was based on the concept of *kō chi kōmin* (kohh-chee kohh-meen), in which all of the people literally belonged to the emperor, had no inherent freedoms, and could not own private property. This system lasted until the eighth century AD.

The foundation of the social system during this period was harmony, or *wa* (wah) in Japanese. This was a hierarchical harmony that required each individual, regardless of his or her place in the vertical structure, to do exactly what was expected in the exact manner prescribed. The absolutes in system were peace and a minutely detailed respect—all within the context of the superior-inferior structure of the society.

The cultural "glue" that was designed to uphold Japanese-style harmony eventually came to be subsumed in the word *amae* (ah-my), which I define as "indulgent love." In this framework, all relationships should be based on a kind of "love" that indulges people's needs as well as their idiosyncrasies, even when it is disadvantageous to do so. The *amae* factor in Japanese relationships was rooted in the desire to avoid disharmony and became a key element in the etiquette of the Japanese, protecting and sustaining their *kao* (kah-oh) or "face"—their sense of honor and their reputation—by making it possible for them to maintain *wa*.

The concern with face in Japanese society gave rise to another important element in Japan's system of etiquette—*enryo* (inn-rio), which literally means "considering from a distance" but in practical usage means holding back, not being aggressive. The avoidance of confrontation and aggression is still very much in evidence today, especially during business meetings, lectures, and other situations where most Americans or Europeans would feel free to speak up with questions or criticisms.

In the system of etiquette that evolved around these cultural imperatives, *wa* was of ultimate importance. All behavior and all relationships—personal, public, and professional—were controlled by a carefully prescribed etiquette that was designed to maintain harmony and often took precedence over both human feelings and practical reasoning.

To hear many older Japanese tell it, *wa* remains the basic building block of Japanese society and has been responsible for much of its economic success. Many Japanese cultural traits, including decision-making by consensus, groupism, shared responsibility, and even ongoing resistance and criticism of the inroads being made by foreign cultures, are predicated on the need and desire for purely Japanese-style harmony.

Having been conditioned over the centuries to a codified system of behavior that took on the color and force of a religion, the Japanese became so accustomed to a specific "Japanese way" of doing things that they developed an extreme sensitivity to any deviation from the norm. Unexpected or nonstandard behavior not only disrupted the cultural imperative of harmony, it was extremely stressful and could be dangerous to the individuals concerned.

Japanese today are still extraordinarily sensitive to non-Japanese behavior. This sensitivity and ensuing stress were partially responsible for the general resistance to foreign companies and foreign workers coming into the country that existed until recent times, and also affected Japanese travel abroad. During the 1950s and 1960s some Japanese who traveled for business were so unprepared to handle the kind of casual, chaotic behavior that Westerners took for granted that they became nervous wrecks after only a short period of time. Many of them holed up in their hotel rooms for several days and then returned home. (Also key was that their hosts often insisted on serving them frequent and large helpings of meat, to which they were not accustomed and which typically made them ill.)

Another important aspect of harmonized behavior in Japan was that it made life predictable. Japanese people could anticipate one another's attitudes and reactions to the point that verbal communication was often unnecessary. The Japanese eventually came to pride themselves on this "telepathic" ability, pointing to it as one of the cultural characteristics that made them different from other people—and made their culture superior in many respects.

Since Japan's cultural telepathy is generally etiquette-based, it is incomprehensible or even unrecognizable to anyone not intimately familiar with Japanese behavior. Anyone—visitor or resident businessperson—who wants to truly understand and communicate with the Japanese must learn to appreciate many aspects of their etiquette.

3

The Vertical Society

Early Japanese society was divided into distinct classes that were arranged in descending order of power and privilege. At the top of the pyramid was, of course, the emperor, followed by members of the royal family, court officials, Shinto priests and Buddhist monks, members of the military, scholars, artisans, farmers, and merchants.

The social system was a vertically arranged hierarchy of superiors and inferiors in which very specific kinds of behavior were required to demonstrate and maintain social differences and to cater to the vanity of those on higher levels of the pyramid. The common people had few rights and were subject to the wishes and whims of the ruling classes.

Rural commoners were required to behave in a submissive and obedient manner toward their clan lords and their lords' samurai retainers. Townspeople were expected to be equally subservient to the town magistrates and their samurai police.

This hierarchical structure meant that members of the upper classes had virtually absolute power over members of the lower classes. Access to an impartial authority higher than a samurai warrior or local warlord was rare, with the result that the common people became resigned to their lot and obedient to those in authority.

As in most feudalistic societies, classes in Japan became hereditary and were eventually fixed by law. The last legal sanctions involving divisions by class, rank, or other criteria were abolished during the first months of the American military occupation of Japan after World War II, but some of the customs were so deeply rooted in the Japanese psyche that they continued.

Strict hierarchies are still a fundamental part of virtually every Japanese organization today, and are sometimes credited with Japan's many successes over the past fifty years. The existence of these hierarchies generally helps to maintain a team approach that is indeed a source of strength—even though many in the internationalized younger generation chafe under such restraints.

4

Samurai Legacies

European countries had their age of knights and professional warriors by other names, but no country in the world was more influenced by the ethics and etiquette of its warrior class than Japan. The famed samurai came to power in AD 1192 with the establishment of a shogunate form of government—essentially a military dictatorship—that was to reign supreme for more than six hundred years.

Japan's central government during this time was ruled over by a series of shoguns who were supported by an army of samurai warriors, as were each of the more than two hundred provincial clan lords around the country. The only citizens permitted to carry weapons and hold office, the samurai followed a code of behavior and belief based on Confucian concepts and Zen principles. They developed a lifestyle centered on the use of the sword, total loyalty to their masters, and a system of formal etiquette that was prescribed down to the slightest bodily movement.

So powerful was the samurai class that their style of living and exquisitely choreographed etiquette became the role model for all Japan. Over the generations, the culture they developed came to impact every aspect of the lives of the Japanese people—their philosophical and spiritual beliefs, their etiquette, their family life, their dress, their work, their aesthetic sense, and even their recreation. This samurai code also had a profound influence on Japanese crafts, literature, poetry, and other artistic and intellectual pursuits that made up the common culture.

The influence of the elite samurai class was even to outlast the shogunate form of government, which was overthrown in 1867 by a group of samurai from distant provinces who were convinced that it was not capable of protecting the country from rising European powers. These ex-samurai rebels took the lead in converting the country from a feudalistic agricultural state into what by the early decades of the twentieth century would be one of the world's foremost industrial powerhouses.

It was also the legacy of the samurai spirit that made it possible for tiny, resource-poor Japan to grow into the world's second largest economy less than 30 years after the disastrous Pacific War (1941–1945) resulted in the distruction of most of its industrial infrastructure.

The samurai and their code of ethics imbued the Japanese people with a range of lasting national traits that included the abilities to use both the emotional and intellectual sides of their brains, to work diligently as teams for the benefit of the group, to focus on ambitious goals with laser-like intensity, to persevere in the face of seemingly insurmountable challenges, and to create arts and crafts that have emotional and sensual appeal as well as practical applications.

The influence of the samurai has diminished today, but it is still visible in the stylized behavior of the Japanese and in the dedication of artists, crafts people, and ordinary workers in Japan. The samurai code of ethics and etiquette still sets the standard that many Japanese strive to attain in their lives. And today there is a growing nostalgia in Japan for the discipline and manners that characterized the lives of the samurai.

5

Language in
Japanese Etiquette

The importance of etiquette in the Japanese worldview had a fundamental influence on the development and use of the Japanese language. The sensitivity of the Japanese to superior-inferior relationships, to the imperative that they pay calculated respect and obsequiousness to superiors in word as well as deed, made them obsessively sensitive to language.

Over the centuries, special words, special word endings, and several different "levels" of the Japanese language emerged as part of the overall etiquette system.

A highly stylized level of language was used at the imperial court, and a lower level was used at the courts of the shogun and the provincial lords. There was also a formal level used when addressing superiors and a distinctive form used in speechmaking, formal writing, and news reporting, as well as levels for addressing equals and inferiors.

These levels of the Japanese language are still in use today and are sufficiently distinct to be considered quasi-dialects. Although the average Japanese person can understand most of these "dialects" fairly well simply from exposure to them from childhood, skill in using them does not come automatically. Each of them has its own vocabulary and style and requires substantial study and practice to master.

In addition, the residents of several regions have their own true dialects of the Japanese language. Special groups and classes of people—including Japan's professional gangster class, the *yakuza* (yah-kuu-zah)—also have their own jargon. Some of these dialects and jargons are so different from standard Japanese that an outsider cannot understand them.

Another important aspect of language etiquette in Japan is the constant use of *aizuchi* (aye-zoo-chee), or what can be loosely translated as "agreement interjections." This refers to the Japanese custom of regularly and systematically agreeing with or acknowledging other people's speech by nodding or saying things such as *hai* (high, meaning "Yes"), *sō desu ka?* (soh dess kah, meaning "Is that right?"), and *ah sō?* (ah soh, meaning "Really!").

These *aizuchi* interjections are expected and needed by the Japanese. If they are not forthcoming, the speaker knows immediately that something is wrong and that the person to whom they are speaking is angry or disagrees to the extent that he or she is deliberately breaking a sanctified custom. Japanese-speaking foreigners unfamiliar with the importance of *aizuchi* may send unintended messages if they fail to follow through with the appropriate interjections.

All told, the role of language in Japan's system of etiquette is central to proper behavior and is the key to getting "inside" the culture. Included in the back of this book are institutionalized Japanese words and phrases pertaining to various situations covered in this guide. By learning when and how to use them, you can greatly improve your ability to communicate successfully with the Japanese.

6

The Use of Names

All family and given names in Japan consist of two or more of the syllables listed at the beginning of this book. When written in kanji, each of the words or syllables in a name has its own ideogram.

Two of the primary characteristics of Japan's traditional etiquette system were its formality and the important role it played when dealing with officialdom. This gave rise to the custom of restricting the use of given names and instead using last names in a formal manner, even in casual and intimate situations. Even today, this custom is usually followed by adults.

Parents address their children by their first names, and children and young people who are close friends use first names and nicknames among themselves. Teenagers, who generally make their own rules wherever they live, may call one another by abbreviated first names, nicknames, or family names, depending on the nature of their relationships.

Although they may have referred to each other using their first names as children, as people grow older they usually begin to use last names when they address each other. Even today adults who are unrelated habitually call each other by their last names no matter how long they may have been acquaintances or friends.

Nowadays dating couples generally use each other's first names or, more correctly, diminutives of their first names.

The use of diminutives is in fact common among close friends and family members in Japan, because many Japanese first names consist of two or more syllables that are awkward or bothersome to pronounce. This is especially true of male names, which may be made up of unusual combinations of four to eight syllables. Some common male given names are Nobuyuki, Mutsuo, Mizumoto, Katsuhiko, Takayoshi, and Hirokazu.

Female given names, on the other hand, have traditionally been easier to say and remember. Among the more common names are Mariko, Sachiko, Kimiko, Teruko, and Minako. In recent decades, parents have begun to give their daughters more distinctive names, without the common "ko" at the end, such as Kazue, Miya, Maya, and Fujie.

Diminutives are nonetheless common among family or close friends of both genders. They may be attached to the first syllable or two of first names only along with the word *chan* (chahn). Adding *chan* to a first name or nickname is the Japanese equivalent of changing Robert to Bobbie or Rebecca to Becky.

Here are some examples of common first names and their diminutives:

Kiyoshi—Ki-chan (kee-chahn)
Yasunori—Yasu-chan or Ya-chan (yah-chahn)
Tomoko—Tomo-chan (toe-moe-chahn)
Minoru—Mi-chan (me-chahn)

The word *chan* may be appended to first names by parents and other adults when speaking to children, and by children when speaking to their parents, grandparents, older brothers and sisters, and others who are close to them, including friends their own age. As a foreigner in Japan, you may address babies and young children using their first names and the word *chan.*

Diminutives for referring to people by their titles also make use of *chan,* as in the following examples.

Father—*O-Tō-chan* (Oh-toh-chahn)
Mother—*O-Kā-chan* (Oh-kaah-chahn)
Grandmother—*O-Bā-chan* (Oh-baah-chahn)
Grandfather—*O-Jii-chan* (Oh-jeee-chahn)

Titles have historically been important replacements for first names, even in marital relationships. In the past Japanese husbands called their wives *o-mae* (oh-my) or *kimi* (kee-me), both of which are forms of "you." After they had children, they referred to their wives as *o-kā-san* (oh-kaah-sahn), meaning "mother" or "mama." In turn, wives did not use their husbands' first names. Instead, they called them *anata* (ah-nah-tah), which in this case is similar to "dear." After having children, wives called their husbands *o-tō-san* (oh-toe-sahn), which translates as "father" or "papa."

These aspects of etiquette in Japan have changed over the past few decades. It is now common for younger husbands and wives, particularly those born after 1960, to use first names in addressing each other. Once they have children, however, they are still likely to refer to each other as "mother" and "father," just as Westerners do when talking to their children.

As in the United States and elsewhere, many unrelated people share family names in Japan. Among the most common of these names are Sato (Sah-toh), Suzuki (Suu-zoo-kee), Takahashi (Tah-kah-hah-she), Tanaka (Tah-nah-kah), and Watanabe (Wah-tah-nah-bay).

Another characteristic of Japanese family names is their frequent incorporation of words such as *yama* ("mountain"), *ta* ("rice field"), *shima* ("island"), *mura* ("village"), *hashi* ("bridge"), *naka* ("between"), *shita* ("below"), and *kawa* ("river").

Although the use of names in Japan is being gradually Americanized and more and more Japanese are beginning to use the first names of new and old foreign friends, last names are always used in formal situations and by people who don't know each other well. In the world of business, it is still unusual for a middle-aged or older Japanese businessperson to call a Japanese colleague by his or her first name, as Westerners commonly do.

Foreign visitors should exercise caution in addressing older Japanese people by their first names unless specifically asked to do so, or the Japanese person has adopted a Western first name and uses it when introducing him- or herself to you. (Generally, Japanese people with foreign names have taken them specifically for use by their foreign friends and acquaintances.)

In business settings, it is always wise to use last names when other Japanese people are present, even if speaking to someone who has a Western first name. In a group situation referring to an individual businessperson with a foreign first name is likely to be interpreted as showing a degree of familiarity or intimacy that is not appropriate.

Among adults in the business world, the honorific *san* (sahn) is invariably attached to whatever name is used when referring to or addressing someone. It is added to names and titles to show respect, almost like the Japanese equivalent of Mr., Mrs., or Miss. It is used when talking to both men and women.

This honorific is also used in written business communications, unless you are writing to someone you know very well.

Visitors to Japan are advised to add _san_ to the first names as well as the last names of older children and adult Japanese they address. It is now little more than a politeness, but nevertheless important.

7

Using Titles

Another key factor in the vertically arranged Japanese society is the importance of titles. Titles were used to rank people within the hierarchy of their group as well as to designate the classification or category of their work or profession.

In feudalistic, samurai-dominated Japan it became the custom to refer to people by their titles instead of their names. This exalted the title instead of the individual and helped maintain the hierarchical relationship between the various classes and between the categories of activity within those classes.

Given the depersonalization of the individual in favor of the group, titles tended to take on an entity of their own and to take precedence over the individuals temporarily bearing them.

Even today, the use of titles—both personal and professional—remains one of Japan's key social graces. Here are some of the most common everyday titles:

Bartender—*Bā tenda* (bah-tane-dah)
Buddhist monk—*O-Bō-san* (oh-boh-sahn)

Butcher—*Nikuya-san* (nee-kuu-yah-sahn), or "Mr. Meat Man"

Carpenter—*Daiku-san* (dike-sahn), or "Mr. Carpenter"

Cook—*Kuuk san* (cook sahn)

Customer, guest, or visitor—*O-Kyaku-san* (oh-kyack-sahn), "Mr. Guest" or "Mr. Customer." *O-Kyaku-sama* (oh-kyack-sah-mah) is an even more polite form of address. This title can be used when referring to both men and women.

Doctor—*O-isha-san* (oh-ee-shah-sahn), or "Mr. Doctor"

Driver (of a taxi or private car)—*Untenshu-san* (uun-ten-shoe-sahn), or "Mr. Driver"

Policeman—*O-Mawari-san* (oh-mah-wah-ree-sahn)

Postman—*Yubinya san* (Yuu-bean-yah-sahn)

School principal—*Kō chō sensei* (kohh-chohh sen-say-e)

Senior (in school, work, and so on)—*Senpai* (sen-pie)

Shinto priest—*Kannushi-san* (kahn-nuu-she-sahn)

Train conductor—*Shasho-san* (shah-show-sahn)

Waiter—*Weta* (way-tah)

Waitress—*Wetoresu* (way-toe-ray-suu)

Young woman (single)—*o-jō-san* (oh-joe-sahn), or "Miss Young Lady"

Your husband—*Go-shujin* (go-shuu-jeen)

Your wife—*Oku-san* (oak-sahn)

Titles are especially important in Japan's business world. The way Americans might refer to the president of their country as "Mr. President" is a good illustration of how the Japanese use titles in business and in the professions. Here are some examples of business titles.

Chairman of the board—*Kaichō* (kye-choe)

President—*Shachō* (shah-choe)

Vice president—*Fuku-shachō* (fuu-kuu-shah-choe)

Senior (executive) managing director—*Senmu* (sem-muu)

Executive managing director—*Jōmu* (joe-muu)

Department manager (general manager)—*Būcho* (buu-choe)

Deputy general manager of the department—*Būcho dairi* (buu-choe die-ree). When addressing a deputy manager, only use *dairi*.

Section manager—*Kachō* (kah-choe)

Deputy section manager—*Kachō dairi* (kah-choe die-ree)

Supervisor—*Kakari-cho* (kah-kah-ree-choe)

It is not essential that foreign visitors to Japan conform to the custom of using titles instead of names in business situations, but by doing so they demonstrate knowledge and appreciation of Japanese customs and are able to communicate more clearly. There is also the personal satisfaction of doing things the "right way," not to mention that using titles often allows you to politely address someone directly and personally without knowing his or her name—or avoid misusing it if you can't pronounce it properly.

8

When & How to Bow

The bow (*o-jigi* / oh-jee-ghee) is the traditional Japanese method of expressing greetings, saying farewell, paying respect, apologizing, showing humility, and indicating understanding and acceptance.

The custom of bowing, which is common to many societies, probably derived from the animalistic behavior of demonstrating submissiveness by lowering the head or dropping to the ground to avoid conflict with stronger adversaries. In any event, it became an institutionalized form of etiquette in religiously oriented societies where such behavior was considered proper when in the presence of deities and their earthly representatives.

As with so many other behavioral traits, the Japanese took the practice of bowing much further than most societies, developing it to a fine art and making it the only acceptable act in many different social situations. During feudal times, failing to bow at the expected time or bowing improperly to a samurai or lord could result in a death sentence, sometimes carried out on the spot.

Historically, training in bowing began before babies could walk; their mothers would push their heads and trunks down repeatedly on the numerous daily occasions when bowing was the proper protocol. By the time children had reached school age, bowing was automatic, almost instinctive. The educational system and the maturing process honed bowing know-how, making it an integral part of the Japanese personality and character.

There are three specific types of bow: the light bow, the medium bow, and the deep bow.

The last, called *sai-keirei* (sigh-kay-ray), or "highest form of salutation," was commonly used during the feudal period but has grown increasingly unusual ever since. After the downfall of the last shogun it was for the most part used only toward the emperor. And with the democratization of Japan following World War II, the emperor renounced his divinity and the use of the *sai-keirei* to pay obeisance to him gradually declined. Except for traditionalists—who are usually elderly—the emperor is now treated like any other dignitary by most Japanese people. When greeting him a medium bow has come to be entirely proper.

In the medium or formal bow the arms are extended downward with the hands resting on the legs above the knees. The body is then bent to about a 45-degree angle. The longer the bow is held the more meaning it has. In a normal situation it is held for only two or three seconds.

During the light bow, the bow most often used today, the body is bent to an approximately 20-degree angle and the bow is held for only a second or so. The hands should be down at the sides when executing the light bow, but there are numerous occasions when this is impractical, such as when you are carrying something. The position of the hands has thus become more or less incidental, although it is polite to make an effort to bring them down to your sides.

Generally speaking, the medium bow is used when greeting dignitaries, when meeting those who are significantly senior to you and to whom you want to show a special degree of respect, and when expressing especially strong feelings of humility, sorrow, or apology to someone.

If you are in a situation where you encounter the same dignitaries or highly placed seniors several times in one day, you should greet them with a medium bow the first time you meet them that day and a light bow thereafter.

The influence of the bow in Japanese society is so powerful that foreign residents who are studying the language and associate frequently with Japanese are susceptible to picking up the custom by osmosis. I sometimes catch myself bowing when I am talking to a Japanese person on the telephone!

Years ago, young Japanese mothers virtually gave up the custom of teaching their children how and when to bow from their toddler days. Nowadays, children are required to bow in school and on numerous other social occasions, but the practice is not being instilled into their reflexes or psyche as it was in the past. Young people entering the work force after the 1980s, especially those entering the retail service industries, had to be taught to bow as part of their company training.

But the bow remains a vital part of daily life and work in Japan, and it is not likely to disappear within the foreseeable future even though the younger generations are assuming a much more casual attitude toward it. There is, in fact, a pronounced tendency among Japanese to gradually revert to traditional attitudes and forms of behavior as they age. They find many of the old customs more satisfying and fulfilling than practices copied from the West.

The foreign visitor does not have to be overly concerned about when and how to bow when dealing with Japanese. Once again, Japanese regard the bow as a custom of their own particular culture and tend to believe that foreigners cannot be expected to do it properly, although in very formal situations they may regard not making any attempt at all as impolite or arrogant.

Bowing is an area of Japanese etiquette that is easy for foreigners to follow when they are introduced to someone and when they are participating in ceremonies or events where bowing is customary. The best rule to follow in a one-on-one situation is to bow when the Japanese do and to be wary of bowing too low or for too long when the occasion does not call for it. It is better to err on the conservative side to avoid being considered insincere or foolish.

Customers at department stores and other public places are not expected to return all of the bows of store employees, but the bows of receptionists in company lobbies should be acknowledged with a slight nodding of the head. A casual nod of the head is also all that is usually called for in more traditional hotels and restaurants, places where the staff regularly bows to guests.

Keep in mind that deep, long bows are reserved for occasions when one demonstrates extraordinary appreciation, respect, humility, or sorrow. Again, older people, especially longtime friends who do not see each other often, will typically bow deep and long as a way of expressing deeply felt emotions. When such bows involve old friends, they are the Japanese equivalent of a warm embrace.

It is still common in many Japanese companies for managers in sections and departments to make a variety of announcements or a short speech each morning to the assembled employees, at the end of which all perform the traditional *cho-rei* (cho-ray-ee), or "morning bow."

9

Shaking Hands
the Japanese Way

The Western custom of shaking hands has been widely accepted in Japan—but although done in virtually all segments of Japanese society, it has not replaced the traditional bow or reduced the bow's overall importance.

Many Japanese use a smooth combination of bowing and shaking hands. There are, however, specific situations when the bow takes precedence over the handshake. These include formal events, especially those involving groups of people and dignitaries when shaking hands with each individual is not practical.

Seemingly all Japanese people, including women, now automatically shake hands with foreigners. They may also combine a handshake with a bow when meeting foreigners for the first time, especially if they are interested in establishing a business relationship with them. In this case the bow serves to demonstrate additional politeness and sincerity. However, Japanese generally dispense with the bow altogether when meeting someone they know or during informal and casual occasions.

Of course, when someone offers his or her hand immediately, it is perfectly all right to take it. However, you should try to have the presence of mind to do it the Japanese way, either by taking the lead or instantly following the other person's lead if he or she begins reaching for a name-card instead of extending a hand.

A growing number of Japanese in international business are totally familiar with Western behavior. They do not bow to foreigners or expect foreigners to bow to them. The behavior of these individuals is obvious enough that the question of whether or not to bow never comes up.

10

The Protocol of Seating

As already noted, Japanese society was traditionally arranged vertically, with superiors placed over inferiors in a hierarchy of ranks that extended from the emperor above to the lowest commoner below. Gradations were minutely defined and separations were meticulously maintained. The seating and line-up of people demonstrated such things as class, rank, age, and gender.

In any situation involving two or more people, the senior or ranking individual took, or was given, the seat of honor. This, of course, is a custom in virtually all societies, but as usual in Japan it was carried to an extraordinary length.

In any semiformal situation, from a photo session to a casual meeting in a coffee shop, restaurant, or company conference room, a Japanese group will typically sort itself out according to real or perceived rank and give the *kami-za* (kah-me-zah), or "seat of honor," to the ranking person or guest. When there are foreign visitors in the group, one of the Japanese will invariably assume a leadership role and direct them to the seats regarded as appropriate for their rank and the occasion.

In any room, the place of honor is usually the seat (or desk or table) farthest from the entrance and located at what might be called the "head" of the room. In a room with a window or windows on only one side, that side is generally designated as the head of the room. The seats of honor should face the door or entrance.

There is also a position of honor in an elevator (in the center nearest the back wall), in a car (the backseat behind the driver), at a head table (in the center of the table away from and opposite the door), in a train coach (the window seat or the center seat), in the first-class cabin of an airplane (a window seat about mid-cabin, on the right side away from the door), when walking with a group (the center of the group), and so on.

When your hosts are Japanese, it is proper to let them designate where you should sit. It is very improper to take the initiative and seat yourself in the place of honor, as ignorant visitors sometimes inadvertently do. If you are the host, it is very important that you direct the ranking Japanese guest to the seat or place of honor and not accept any show of reluctance on his or her part, even if you have to use some degree of playful force.

In public places such as theaters or open seating on trains, you can "save" a seat by leaving an article of clothing or some other possession on it, generally without being concerned that it might be stolen.

11

Dining Etiquette

Perhaps no other area in the lives of ordinary Japanese has been more carefully prescribed or ritualized than the simple process of eating. As a result of the overall cultural emphasis on defining, classifying, categorizing, and systemizing everything, the early Japanese turned the preparation, presentation, and consumption of food into a ritualized experience that was both aesthetic and culinary.

Meals at the imperial court, at the court of the shogun, in the castles of the provincial lords, in the homes of ranking samurai, in Buddhist temples, at traditional inns, and in the homes of well-to-do merchants were exquisite exercises in stylized service and beautiful blends of colors, textures, and tastes as carefully choreographed as a Kabuki play.

The beauty of the food, the artistic complement of the tableware, the formal manner of the service, and the proper dining etiquette were considered among the highest levels of cultural expression, indicative of one's character and refinement.

The centuries-long devotion of Japan's upper class to such formal dining naturally influenced the lower classes, but the custom of ritualized dining was primarily brought to the masses by a political policy beginning in the 1600s.

In the late 1630s, the third Tokugawa shogun decreed an "alternate attendance" policy that required nearly all of the country's more than 270 provincial lords to keep their families in the shogun's capital of Edo (present-day Tokyo) at all times. The lords themselves, along with their large retinues of servants and samurai guards, were required to spend every other year in Edo in attendance at the court of the shogun.

This policy meant that a constant stream of visitors traveled to and from Edo on foot throughout the year, as the clan lords with their guards, servants, and retainers made the semi-annual trek from their domains to the capital. Immediately after this edict went into effect, inns sprang up every few miles along the five main roads to Edo to accommodate the masses of travelers. There were three classes of inns: luxury inns for the lords and their personal attendants; first-class inns for their ranking retainers; and ordinary inns for foot soldiers, lower-ranking retainers, and other travelers.

Implemented as a security measure to prevent provincial lords from attempting to overthrow the government, the alternate attendance system continued for some 250 years, influencing the spread of court-style dining not only in the thousand inns throughout the country, but also in restaurants and in the homes of wealthy merchants.

Other travelers on the roads included a steady stream of entertainers, gamblers, sumo wrestlers, and itinerant priests. Also during the early years of the Tokugawa period, religious associations called *kō* (kohh) began a system of collecting money from members and then drawing lots to see who went on pilgrimages to famous shrines and temples around the country. This system added greatly to the number of travelers using the new network of inns.

Present-day inns and traditional restaurants continue to emulate the preparation and serving style that evolved during the long Tokugawa era (1603–1867)—many of them offering exactly those dishes that were enjoyed by the emperors, shoguns, clan lords, and ranking people of the past. Dining Japanese-style at a restaurant in one of the beautiful inns that still dot the country remains one of the special joys of visiting Japan.

Though eating Japanese-style remains highly ritualized, the visitor can get by with a minimum of skill in using *o-hashi* (oh-hah-she), or chopsticks, the basics of eating etiquette, and in many cases the ability to sit on the floor for an extended period.

If it is your first time with *o-hashi*, it's a good idea is to ask for a few instructions on how to hold them. If you still have difficulty using them as tongs to grasp pieces of food, just hold the ends close together and use them as a scoop. Many Japanese meals are served in bowls that can be—and often are—picked up and held close to the chin while eating.

One technique you can borrow from the Japanese is to pick up your rice bowl and use it as a tray or "safety net" when conveying food to your mouth with chopsticks. It is also common for people to hold their free hand under the tidbit of food being conveyed to the mouth with *o-hashi*. This is especially useful when you are eating something relatively large and heavy, such as sushi.

For that matter, however, sushi is picked up by hand as often as it is with chopsticks, and there is nothing wrong with eating it that way. In sushi restaurants and in inns you are typically provided with an *o-shibori* (oh-she-boe-ree), a small dampened cloth, to wipe your hands before and after eating.

Chopstick taboos include sticking them into your rice and leaving them standing up, and using your own chopsticks to serve yourself from a common dish. If serving chopsticks or other utensils are not available, reverse your chopsticks and use the top ends when serving yourself or someone else.

When not in use, chopsticks are customarily placed on small ceramic or bamboo rests. If rests are not provided, lean your chopsticks on the side of a dish or saucer. When you have finished eating, lay the chopsticks across the top of your main dish, plate, or bowl, or across your rice bowl. In formal situations it is proper to lay your chopsticks down when you are being served.

Japanese-style soup is served in small lacquered bowls. You simply pick up the bowl and sip from it as if it were a cup. The ingredients in many such soups settle to the bottom in a matter of seconds and you may stir the soup with your chopsticks before drinking.

In Japanese-style restaurants where diners eat sitting on *tatami* (tah-tah-me) reed-mat floors, it is permissible to ask for a *zaisu* (zah-ee-sue), a legless chair that sits directly on the floor. This is especially helpful when the meal is a banquet lasting for an hour or more. Note, however, that it is usually only in large banquet settings, particularly in inns, that *zaisu* are available.

One marvel of eating out in Japan that impresses Westerners is how simple it usually is to order the specific dish they want. In their usual way of making things as convenient and easy as possible, most Japanese restaurants showcase wax replicas of all the dishes they offer in outside display cases or on tables set up for that purpose. These replicas are so authentic in every respect that many newcomers think they are the real thing and can't resist touching them. The replicas are generally identified with name and price tags so you know what you are going to get and how much it is going to cost before you even enter the restaurant. Some restaurants have identifying numbers on their wax replicas, so you can order by the number.

Also surprising to some Westerners is that by the beginning of the twenty-first century rice had lost its hallowed place as the primary staple of the diet among Japan's young-er generations. It has been replaced by bread rolls and sliced bread that is available in an amazing variety and is among the tastiest in the world.

This phenomenon resulted in Japan's rice farmers mount-ing campaigns to bring young people back to rice-based diets to restore some of their lost market, including creating a vari-ety of breads made from rice flour. However, the importance of rice in the Japanese diet is likely to continue diminishing.

Still, many Japanese diners eat more than one bowl of rice with their meals, and there are many dishes for which the taste of rice and its form and consistency are a natural complement, so it is not likely to completely disappear.

If you like rice with any of your Japanese meals and finish your first bowl early it is normally assumed that you want a refill. If a server doesn't automatically refill your bowl, point to it or lift it up and say *O-Kawari kudasai* (oh-kah-wah-ree kuu-dah-sie), which means "A refill, please." You can also use this sentence to request a refill of your tea cup.

When eating the so-called *kaiseki* (kie-say-kee) type of meals (a light meal made up of a variety of tiny portions that originated in Buddhist temples), rice is normally the last main course served. If you simply must have rice to go with the exotic-looking and exotic-tasting tidbits, apolo-gize and order it by saying *Gohan kudasai* (go-hahh kuu-dah-sie)—"Rice, please."

It is also wise to keep in mind that accidentally wandering into and eating at a *kaiseki* restaurant can get you stuck with a bill that is two or three times higher than what you would pay in an ordinary restaurant. Indulging in the *kaiseki* tradition, as affluent Japanese do often, can be expensive.

12

The Japanese Way
of Drinking

As in most ancient agricultural societies, the Japanese discovered how to turn grain into an alcoholic drink very early in their history. A wine-like beverage called *sake* (sah-kay) made from rice was used as a sacrament in Shinto ceremonies long before recorded history began.

The use of sake as a tonic for older people gradually spread among the population. With full religious sanction, drinking sake eventually became an important component of Japanese society. It was used not only as a medicinal tonic but also for recreational purposes, to commemorate special events such as contracts and weddings, to accompany meals, and so on. All bars, inns, and public restaurants served sake as a matter of course.

The Japanese quickly took to beer and whiskey when these drinks were introduced from the West in the mid-1800s, and soon both drinks became major industries. Sake, however, is still considered the national beverage.

Given the importance of sake and drinking throughout Japanese history, it is not surprising to find that there are numerous points of etiquette applying to drinking. The drinking of alcoholic beverages in Japan today is as institutionalized as drinking tea. Like so many facets of Japanese etiquette, the rules of drinking are far less strictly adhered to these days, but remain influential enough to make ignoring them inconsiderate if not impolite.

The most conspicuous drinking custom in Japan is probably for individuals, especially hosts, to make a special point of pouring drinks for other people in their party, particularly guests. In cabarets, hostess nightclubs, and geisha inns, it is the job of the hostesses or geisha to keep guests' glasses topped off. This, in turn, encourages drinking, because it is customary to take at least one sip from the glass or cup each and every time it is refilled.

However, if you decline the offer of a refill, the worst that will happen is that your reputation as a party animal will go down a notch or two.

Traditional Japanese drinking etiquette called for patrons or guests to hold their glasses or sake cups with both hands when they were being refilled, and also to use both hands when pouring for someone else. This custom is not always followed now, but when it is, it indicates that the person doing it has exceptionally good manners and probably good character, as well.

If you are a guest and the host or some other member of the party pours a drink for you, you should reciprocate—if he or she will let you. Some will strongly resist any such effort, either because they want to emphasize that you are the guest or because they want you to be obligated to them.

Given the Japanese propensity to drink and to expect others to drink, it is often necessary for light drinkers or non-drinkers to draw a line.

Having some kind of illness or weakness that is aggravated by copious drinking can be used fairly effectively to avoid overdrinking. In my case, it is excessively long-lasting hangovers. In Japanese "hangover" is *futsuka-yoi* (futes-kah-yoh-ee), which can be loosely translated as "two-day drunk." I turn this into a joke by saying that I suffer from *mikka-yoi* (meek-kah-yoh-ee), or "three-day drunk," which usually gets me off the hook.

One of the most common ways to limit your drinking is to pretend that you are tipsier than you really are. Japanese habitually feign drunkenness not only to avoid drinking too much but also to give them an excuse to "break etiquette" and do things they wouldn't ordinarily do.

This attitude springs from the level of etiquette the Japanese must follow while sober, which has traditionally been so strict that their real personality and character remained hidden. The one occasion when the Japanese were, and still are, culturally permitted to *bureiko ni suru* (boo-ray-ee-koe nee suu-rue)—or discard the formal etiquette that otherwise controls their lives—is during drinking parties away from home or office. The word *bureiko* by itself means "an informal party." It can also mean "abandon all formalities."

Some Japanese hosts are exceptionally forceful in encouraging guests to drink, and it is often necessary to be strong-willed to resist them. Refusing to drink or drinking only moderately must be done with diplomacy, because the Japanese believe that the only way you can really get to know people is to see how they behave when they are drunk.

Japanese people are still inclined to believe that anyone who refuses to get drunk is hiding something. The best way out of this subtle cultural bind is to drink a little bit and then behave in a casual manner.

A word that virtually all visitors find very useful is the traditional Japanese drinking toast *kanpai* (kahm-pie). As during Western toasts, you hold your drink up in the air and say or shout *kanpai!*

13

Paying Bar &
Restaurant Bills

Japanese are noted for their hospitality and skill as hosts. Steeped in protocol, their banquets and parties are usually stereotyped and rigidly controlled, but once you get beyond the cultural factors, such events with Japanese friends can be wonderful experiences.

Being able to speak Japanese and participate in the jokes and conversation will make any party much better, but Japanese-style parties can be fun even for people who don't speak the language, as long as they are not shy about enjoying themselves.

There is one point of Japanese party protocol that often presents foreign visitors with a dilemma. This is the habit the Japanese have of insisting on paying for restaurant or bar bills, even if that obligation rightfully belongs to the foreigner. I have seen and been personally involved in actual physical struggles to obtain possession of a check.

This behavior has been a national characteristic for centuries, and certainly does not derive from the economic success of the country. It is instead a combination of a strong desire to be hospitable to guests, an expression of pride, and an imperative to gain face for themselves and for

Japan—all characteristics that flowered during the illustrious Tokugawa period.

Tokugawa history abounds with stories of ordinary people going to extremes to extend extraordinary hospitality and outspend others in situations where such displays were strictly for show and the personal satisfaction involved. During that era making profit through commerce was considered the lowest of all callings and the display of affluence was prohibited. In these circumstances, one of the few ways members of the merchant class could demonstrate their business acumen and financial superiority was through profligate spending on entertainment.

Some visitors, confronted with the cost of having fun in Japan, are only too happy to have someone else pick up the tab. That is fine if you are clearly a guest. But if you are the host, or it is obviously your turn to foot the bill, allowing someone else to pay is both unfair and demeaning.

When you should pay the bill (or want to pay it) it is best to pay in advance or leave the party before it ends, pay the bill, and then return. The latter approach is not only the easiest but is also the correct etiquette, because displaying or talking about money is also considered ill-mannered and beneath the dignity of a cultured person.

14

Public Etiquette

For centuries the focus of responsibility in Japan was extremely narrow and limited to the family, the work group, the village, and the local clan authorities. Each unit of this vertical grouping was more or less exclusive and in competition with every other unit.

Japan's clan system pitted the clans against one another and endured until 1870, when it was officially abolished after the downfall of the shogunate government in 1867. This system contributed to the group-against-group mentality common in Japan, as each clan strove to be self-sufficient and to improve its ranking with respect to other clans (goals clearly discernible in Japanese companies today).

The Japanese thus became group-oriented to the point that there was little or no communication or cooperation with other groups. The only way you could become a member of one of these groups was to be born into it or to enter it at the very bottom when young. Outsiders were either ignored or considered potential enemies.

These cultural elements resulted in one of the early contradictions of the Japanese character. On the one hand, Japanese people quickly became renowned for their refined, stylized manners and unfailing courtesy, but on the other hand they were also criticized for being rude in public, uncaring about strangers, and heedless of the environment.

In fact, the negative aspect of this reputation was exaggerated by foreigners who were not really familiar with Japan. They certainly had not experienced the often incredible lengths to which Japanese have traditionally gone in sincere and selfless demonstrations of their honesty and goodwill toward other people and their concern for the environment as a whole.

Caring for the needs of others and one's environment have long been important parts of Japanese culture. During Japan's feudal age, for example, families and shopkeepers swept and picked up around their homes and places of business every morning, resulting in yards and streets being scrupulously clean.

In more recent times, Japanese sociologists and management gurus have pointed out that although the Japanese work exceptionally well within their own groups, they have little or no affinity for working with other groups or taking individual responsibility for things outside of their immediate work area. This observation reflected a post-World War II phenomenon resulting from the frenzy to rebuild Japan after the war, and is no longer accurate. By the last decades of the twentieth century many Japanese people in positions of authority—both public and private—had developed a remarkably progressive public conscious and grown sensitive and responsive to environmental issues. They had also begun to agitate for people to take more personal responsibility.

Today, the Japanese are among the world's most helpful, generous and hospitable people, and their public behavior is far superior to what is common in most other countries.

There is also very little violent crime in Japan. For the most part, people, including women and children, are fairly safe in the streets at all hours of the day and night. On weekends and holidays teenage boys and girls flock to the most notorious entertainment districts, known to be hangouts for organized criminal gangs, without having to worry about their personal safety.

Likewise, theft is normally not an issue in Japan. You can leave possessions such as bicycles out in public day or night and they will not be stolen. You can set your baggage down in transportation terminals, including airports, walk away, and come back later to find them exactly where you left them— although I don't recommend that you do it deliberately.

There are probably more public vending machines in Japan than in most of the rest of the world combined because their owners do not have to worry about them being vandalized.

Public graffiti in Japan is still extremely rare. I vividly recall that I had been riding Tokyo's subways for more than 40 years before I finally saw some—a tiny pencil drawing measuring about half an inch in diameter that someone had scrawled on the wall of a coach next to a door. That was the first and last graffiti that I have seen on public transportation in Japan.

About the worst public nuisance you are likely to encounter in Japan is people who went out after work and had a lot to drink before boarding subways and trains on their way home. They are almost never rowdy or violent, but they sprawl and sleep on the seats and have been known to pester foreigners by trying to talk to them.

As time passes, some aspects of public behavior in Japan have come to resemble what's common in the West. Public displays of affection, once taboo, are now commonplace among the young. They usually involve no more than intertwining arms or holding hands while walking, still relatively tame by Western standards. This may not be the case in parks frequented by the young, however.

Another aspect of public behavior in Japan that has changed dramatically is eating and drinking, especially while walking. Prior to the 1980s, eating and drinking in public were virtually taboo except in the case of food purchased from street vendors and during shrine- and temple-sponsored festivals, where snacks have traditionally been sold from stalls. In the past, patrons of the many street vendors, common in Japan since ancient times, generally ate before leaving the area or took their purchases home with them. (Eating and drinking on long-distance buses and trains has also been the custom since the appearance of these conveyances, but that was not considered public behavior.)

Young people began ignoring the general taboo against eating in public after the appearance of fast-food outlets that had little or no inside seating. The first McDonald's in Japan, which opened in the entrance foyer of the Mitsukoshi department store in Tokyo's famed Ginza district on July 20, 1971, had no seating at all. Most customers ate while standing or milling around on the sidewalk in front of the shop. Some of the new ice-cream shops also only had service counters fronting on sidewalks.

People eating while walking around in public are still rare enough today to be conspicuous and regarded as ill-mannered by older people, especially if they are not in the immediate vicinity of the food stalls or counter-type restaurants that abound near transportation terminals and on boarding platforms.

Visitors concerned with presenting a good image while in Japan should limit their eating in public to accepted occasions and areas, which include picnics, flower-viewing parties, hiking, while on long-distance train rides and sightseeing buses, as well as in the vicinity of fast-food counters and street vendors.

16

Electronic Etiquette

Future historians may well note that the appearance of computers, access to the Internet, and the proliferation of cell phones in Japan in the last decades of the twentieth century had a much greater and faster impact on the culture and economy of the country than the appearance of the first Western technology in the mid-1500s.

The power these electronic devices derived was so great because they were virtually "culture free"—meaning that they did not require or demand that people using them conform to the rigid forms of personal etiquette that had controlled and severely limited the behavior of the Japanese for generations. Because they were culture free, these devices permeated the economic and social life of the Japanese from top to bottom, causing in a matter of a few years changes that in earlier times would have taken decades or centuries.

The most pervasive and conspicuous of these new devices are mobile or cell phones, called *keitai denwa* (kay-tie den-wah) in Japanese. *Keitai denwa* means "portable telephone" as well as "portable telephones," since there is no distinction between the singular and the plural in Japanese nouns.

The instant popularity of mobile phones among Japanese teenagers in particular was an outgrowth of the paging devices that appeared in the late 1980s and quickly became their primary means of communicating with one another. They used the numerical codes on the devices to phonetically spell out messages. For example, 4-6-4-9 translated as *yo-ro-shi-ku* ("hello," or "best regards"); 3-3-4-1 translated as *sa-mi-shi-i* ("I'm lonely").

Today, virtually all teenagers and adults in Japan have cell phones that include a wide range of features well beyond verbal communication and text messaging, including cameras, Internet browsers, access to television broadcasts and live video feeds, games, GPS navigation, music players, barcode scanners, phone and address books, calculators, alarm clocks and stopwatches, calendars, note pads, sub-sites for checking train and airline schedules, and electronic systems for paying for purchases and subway and train fares.

All cell phones also have a "silent mode" (known as "public mode" or "manners mode" in Japanese) that is designed to be engaged when using a phone would be not only impolite but a serious imposition on others. Silent mode is intended for public places, including buses, subways, trains, theaters, meeting halls, libraries, hospitals, and so on.

There are signs in subway and train cars admonishing passengers to turn their cell phones off. It is important to obey these signs, especially on long-distance trains, because it is common for people to doze and sleep when using public transportation. On other occasions and in other places visitors should be guided by their common sense—will the use of a cell phone disturb others? If so, it should be avoided.

This said, as in other countries many Japanese people ignore both signs and common courtesy in their use of cell phones, causing an ongoing public debate about this kind of environmental "sound pollution."

At the time of this writing, most foreign-made cell phones will not work in Japan because they are based on different technologies. This has resulted in several Japanese companies establishing cell phone rental counters at international airports and other sites within the country for the benefit of visitors. Rental fees are modest enough and in some cases the phones may be returned by mail if the traveler is not going to pass by one of the company's rental facilities when leaving the country. Names of cell phone rental companies and locations of their outlets are available on the Internet.

It can be very important for visitors in Japan to have cell phones because public telephones have become increasingly scarce in the country. It is also not always convenient or possible for visitors to reach operators who speak their native tongue when using what phones are available. Phone numbers that might come in handy while you are in Japan can be loaded into *keitai denwa,* and if you are traveling with family or friends the phones make it possible for you to stay in touch with each other.

Fax and e-mail etiquette depends on the relationship between the senders and receivers. Bilingual and internationalized Japanese use the same basic etiquette that is common among other people—polite titles and forms of speech for seniors and other important people and ordinary forms of address and vocabulary for close friends.

Attaching the honorific *san,* or Mr., to last names is still common among people who are strangers as well as those who know each other but are not on a close-friend level. The Japanese often attach *san* to the first names of foreign friends they write to. This is also a good practice for foreigners to follow in addressing correspondence to their Japanese acquaintances and friends.

International hotels in Japan have Internet connections in all of their rooms, and some, like the very high-tech

Peninsula Hotel, have complimentary cell phones in their suites that guests may use during their stay.

Visitors who do not have access to Internet connections in their hotel rooms may make use of a growing number of "Internet cafés" that are typically located on the main floors of major multi-use office buildings. These buildings have restaurant arcades and shops in their basements and on their main floors, and offices on the floors above. An outstanding example of this is the new Marunouchi building across the plaza from Tokyo Central Station. Its restaurant arcades are mid-way up the building, where many of the restaurants provide diners with sweeping views of the Imperial Palace grounds and the city.

16

Using (& Surviving) Public Transportation

Mass transportation in Japan is just that—masses of people pressed into buses, subway coaches, and train cars, particularly during morning and evening rush hours. At these times, most forms of transportation carry from three to four times their rated capacity.

With such huge numbers of people dependent on public transportation, the Japanese have taken advantage of their genius for organization and the latest technologies to develop extraordinarily efficient transportation systems. These systems interconnect bus, subway, and train lines, and facilitate the rapid movement of millions of people throughout the entire country every day.

In the first decade and a half of Japan's postwar democratic period (1945–1960), getting on and off trains was a free-for-all that often left people injured. But as transportation systems improved, the traditional Japanese penchant for order reasserted itself. Despite the increasingly large crowds of commuters, using the system became much safer.

Today, places on boarding platforms where individual coaches stop are clearly marked. Japanese commuters waiting to board subways or local trains line up in an orderly fashion and patiently wait their turn to board. On many sub-way platforms you will see lanes, either painted or embed-ded, that passengers use to line up in.

Nonetheless, visitors should keep in mind that from about 7:30 to 9:30 AM and 5:00 to 7:00 PM the masses of commuters are such that getting in and out of coaches can be a chal-lenge. (Subways and trains fill up again from around 9 to 11 PM, when people who work late and those who go out for dinner and drinks after work begin heading home.)

During the heaviest part of the rush hour, platform work-ers at busier stations literally push passengers onto the cars, packing them in so tightly it is virtually impossible for those standing in the vicinity of the doors to move. In winter heavy clothing results in even more crowding.

Visitors are advised to avoid using public transportation during the worst of the rush hours. If you must travel during these periods, it is best to give yourself a few minutes lee-way. Also, you should not board the train until you are near the front of the line. If you are toward the back, let other waiting commuters pass you and wait for the next train or bus to come.

When waiting to board and the stream of disembarking passengers has stopped, board very quickly and if possible position yourself in one of the corners just inside the door, turning your back to the crowd and holding on so you are not pushed into the middle of the aisle where there is nothing to hold on to. This maneuver will prevent you from being shoved further and further into the coach, reducing the pos-sibility of losing your balance as the car starts and stops and sways from side to side, as well as making it easier to disem-bark when you come to your stop.

There are doors on both sides of the coaches; the side that opens varies from station to station. If you don't know which doors open at your stop and you guess incorrectly (after you have wedged yourself into a door corner), you are usually still better off than if you were packed into the middle of the aisle, where you get buffeted each time there is an exchange of passengers.

On subways and commuter trains there are digital read-out signs above the doors that note, in both English and Japanese, which door is going to open at the station coming up. Some lines and cars also announce the coming stations and which doors are going to open on automated public address systems.

On most transportation lines there are also lists of stations on panels above the coach doors, allowing you to identify your stop in advance and begin working your way toward an exit. If you are caught in the aisle well away from the doors, it is best to do your maneuvering when the train is stopped at a station and other people are pushing their way toward the exits.

Boarding platforms have numerous signs on free-standing signboards and roof pillars that list all of the stations on the line. You should make note of the station where you are to disembark before boarding. The lists on the pillars also include the time from each station to the next.

During rush-hours, the crowding of Japan's transportation system results in close, prolonged body contact among standing passengers. Proper etiquette in this situation is to keep your hands still, remain as passive as possible, and avoid direct eye contact. Some people read if there is enough room to hold reading material. Many keep their eyes closed, and some of those who are sitting fall asleep.

In Tokyo and other cities you can save time and avoid having to find the fare for each of your destinations by purchasing commuter passes that are good for various lengths of time. These passes are available from the offices in main stations.

First-time visitors to Japan should keep in mind that the left rear doors of taxis (the ones on the sidewalk side) are automated and both opened and closed by the drivers, so you need to stand out of the way when preparing to enter a taxi. Once in the taxi, allow the driver to close the door.

It is not customary to tip taxi drivers in Japan, but if they help you load and unload an unusual amount of baggage, tipping is a nice gesture.

17

Bath & Toilet Protocol

Most visitors to Japan are curious about bathing etiquette because they have heard stories of public baths and mixed-sex bathing, or have perhaps seen titillating scenes in movies such as *Shogun*. These may have resulted in prospective visitors conjuring up scenes of sexual behavior in Japan's *o'furo* (Oh-fuu-roh), or baths. Actually, the Japanese have never associated premarital or extramarital sex with "sin" in the Christian sense. Sex was considered a natural function, and nudity in its proper place, such as the bath, was not regarded as licentious, suggestive, sinful, scandalous, or anything else.

When foreign missionaries first arrived in Japan in the 1540s, they were horrified by the Japanese custom of bathing regularly and bathing in groups. Europeans at that time believed that bathing more than once or twice a year was harmful to one's health. The fact that Japanese men and women bathed together was even more of a shock.

At first the missionaries tried to totally prohibit their new Japanese converts from bathing. When this didn't work they gave them permission to bathe every two weeks. This also failed, so they finally approved of weekly bathing. Among other results of the ignorance and arrogance of these early missionaries to Japan was that they and their Japanese converts smelled bad.

Missionaries were expelled from Japan in the late sixteenth and early seventeenth centuries and were not allowed back in until after the fall of the Tokugawa shogunate in the 1860s. But the missionary orders that flocked back to the newly re-opened Japan had not learned anything about the human condition in the intervening centuries. Once back in Japan they continued their opposition to Japanese-style bathing.

The age-old Japanese custom of daily bathing in large public baths as well as in private baths survived both missionaries and other social changes until the early 1950s, when female Japanese members of the new postwar democratic Diet prevailed on the government to pass legislation making it mandatory for public bathhouses to segregate the sexes. (For the first year or so many bathhouses conformed to this new law by stringing a rope across the middle of the bathing areas.)

However, the new mixed-bathing taboo did not apply to private baths in homes, hotels, inns, or spas, where mixed-sex bathing continues today.

While in Japan, you might encounter a number of different kinds of bathrooms and bathing facilities.

Inn Bathrooms

Experiencing a Japanese-style bath at an inn is one of the special pleasures of life in Japan, especially when the bath is in one of the more than two thousand hot-spring spas (*onsen* / own-sin) in the country. The smallest of these spas are host to five or six inns; larger ones have well over one hundred inns.

Baths must meet government-set standards for mineral content and temperature before they can qualify for the status of hot-spring baths.

The development and use of hot-spring baths in Japan goes back for two thousand or more years, with many of the baths having been in use and famous for centuries. There is copious literature in both Japanese and English listing and describing hot-spring spas throughout the country.

Guests at hot-spring spa inns and other traditional Japanese inns may have a choice of mixed-sex, gender-specific, or private bathing. Baths specifically for families are called *kazoku-buro* (kah-zoe-kuu-buu-roh), or "family baths."

All inns provide their guests with yukata (yuu-kah-tah) robes (these will be in your room when you check in), which are invariably donned by guests as soon as they get to their assigned rooms. The yukata are often worn throughout the visitors' stay at the inn, including when they go out on the grounds of the inn or to the nearest town or city.

Shortly after guests are settled in their rooms they are usually served tea (or beer or sake if they choose) along with some tidbits such as small squares of sweetened bean curd paste. Generally, the next activity is heading to the bath.

The typical inn bath consists of two rooms. First is an anteroom where you remove your yukata and hallway slippers. The anterooms have either wicker baskets or small wall slots for your yukata, slippers, and anything else you brought along. Some also have a supply of small hand-towels called *tenugui* (tay-nuu-gooey), which you may wash with, dry with, and use to cover your genitals when walking around.

Adjoining is the main room, closed off by sliding doors. This room contains the bathtub, which in some inns is as large as a small swimming pool. The baths have tiled floors slanted to drain water and are equipped with hot and cold spigots lining one or more walls; buckets or pans to fill with water; and low stools, plastic or wood, to sit on.

The routine is to first douse yourself with several pans or buckets of water, scrub clean, and then get into the tub or pool to soak. If the bath water is really hot—and in some baths it may be approaching scalding—you may want to douse yourself with a few pans of cold water after getting out of the tub or pool.

Even if the bathwater is very hot, it is not proper or feasible to add cold water to make it more comfortable unless you are in a private bath. Some spa baths are noted for the hot temperature of their bathwater, so it pays to inquire about the water's temperature—or feel it for yourself by sticking a hand into the bath—before climbing in.

In some of the famous inns that have really hot water, there are attendants who coordinate guests getting into (and out of!) the baths to prevent them from over-heating.

Public Bathhouses

Some adventurous visitors to Japan take advantage of neighborhood public baths, or *sento* (sen-toe), where people without baths in their homes go for their daily ablutions. Public bathhouses appeared to be on the verge of becoming obsolete by the 1970s, but the proprietors rallied by adding various new services such as adjoining video-game rooms and coin laundries, and were soon back on their feet. The number of *sento*, however, is definitely on the decline.

Bathing etiquette in Japan's *sento* is quite simple. People going to public baths take their own soap, wash pans, towels, and washcloth. After leaving your clothes in the dressing room, the bathing procedure is essentially the same as at the spas. In winter some people (usually men) "cheat" by merely dousing themselves with several buckets of hot water and entering the tub without scrubbing. After they warm up they get out of the tub, scrub, and then get back in for a final soaking. This, of course, dirties the tub water even though it is being continuously replenished with clean water.

Once out of the tub, sponge off with your *tenugui* (tay-nuu-gooey) washcloth and return to the dressing room to finish drying.

In some older baths and bathhouses the only source of hot water may be the tub itself, in which case there will be a bucket or large dipper on hand to take water out of the tub for dousing yourself, washing, and rinsing.

Another part of Japan's "public bathing" industry—officially known as "soaplands" (or saunas in Nagoya)—is actually part of the country's unofficial sex industry. Although most are geared toward men, a few of the soaplands cater exclusively to female clientele. If you know what to look for you can spot several dozen soaplands, which were formerly known as "Turkish baths," strung along the freeway from Tokyo's Narita International Airport to the central areas of the city. There are anywhere from two or three to dozens of them in the larger entertainment districts of Tokyo and other cities.

In addition to not being located in residential areas, the soaplands have suggestive names and advertise themselves with neon signs. They are staffed by young women who are formally known as masseuses.

Bathrooms in Private Homes

The typical Japanese home bathroom consists of two small rooms: The entry room for undressing, which is equipped with a sink, mirror, and accessories or medicine cabinet; and the actual bathroom, which is equipped with a shower and a deep bathtub. The tub usually has a paneled cover to help keep the water hot when the tub is not being used.

The shower is separate from the bathtub and consists of a wall-mounted hot-cold faucet that allows you to adjust the temperature of the water and a flexible water hose that you can hold in your hand or fix in a bracket on the wall.

Just as at public baths, if you are going to use the bathtub the custom is to first douse yourself with several buckets of hot water from a wall spigot or the tub, wash yourself, and then get into the tub to soak. You do not—ever!—wash in the tub. The floor of the bathroom is tiled and designed so that the water you use will run off into a drain.

In homes the same bath water is used by the whole family, so it is important to keep it clean. The water is normally changed daily.

Toilet Protocol

In Japan toilets are almost always completely separate from bathrooms. You will come across two types of toilets in Japan—so-called Western-style toilets and the traditional Japanese-style toilets, which you squat over instead of sit on.

All hotels are equipped with Western-style toilets. Most inns have both types, but some older inns may have only Japanese-style. Some long-distance trains and buses have Western-style toilets; others have only Japanese-style toilets.

Public toilets, including those in places such as office buildings, department stores, and train stations, generally have both Western-style and at least one or two Japanese-style toilets. Free-standing public restrooms are likely to have only Japanese-style toilets because they are much more sanitary and easier to keep clean.

All public toilets in Japan are normally equipped with toilet paper, although free-standing public toilets that do not have clean-up crews keeping close watch over them may be out of paper. It is wise to carry a packet of tissue with you, just in case. (At major transportation terminals there are frequently people standing around in front of the exits passing out free packets of tissue paper that carry various advertisements.)

Using a Japanese-style toilet, which requires squatting all the way down, can be a major challenge for some people, and this should be kept in mind. Japanese-style toilets are, in fact, more sanitary than Western-style toilets, and the position they require you to take is more natural for what you need to do.

Keep in mind that when using bathrooms in inns and private homes you should not wear your hallway slippers into them. Special slippers intended for these rooms are placed outside their doors. Leave your slippers in the hallway outside of the toilet, and step into the toilet slippers.

If you have never encountered a Japanese-style toilet before, keep in mind that you squat down facing the low canopy-style "hood" at one end of the ceramic slot—otherwise you are likely to bump into it with your rear-end.

18

The Importance of
Gift Giving

The need to maintain harmony during Japan's feudal era contributed to the Japanese penchant for gift giving on a gargantuan scale. People's rights were not fully protected by law during this time, and the rights of those in power were virtually unrestrained, which resulted in gifts becoming the "oil" that helped society to function smoothly.

Gifts were given by inferiors to superiors or other people in positions of power to build goodwill, maintain good relations, solicit favors, get out of difficulties, and avoid getting on the bad side of anyone in a position to do them harm.

Gift giving, in fact, developed into a highly structured ritual requiring extensive knowledge to perform properly. (At one point, the rules pertaining to giving a gift to a high-ranking member of the shogun's court consisted of over 200 pages of precise instructions.)

In the early centuries, items that came to be prized as gifts included special foods, silk fabrics, and pieces of lacquerware and other handicraft items. Since the method of presentation was as important as the gifts themselves, a whole packaging industry grew up to serve the gift-giving custom. Packaging became refined to the point that it could be considered a fine art.

With the emergence of a more democratic society in Japan following the end of the Pacific War in 1945, gift-giving customs changed. Now, in addition to those occasions when gift giving is still important in making and nurturing good relations and securing favors, it is also practiced by companies on a massive scale as a gesture of goodwill toward customers and as a token of appreciation for past business.

Two annual gift-giving seasons are now so important in the Japanese economy that they make up a significant percentage of the annual sales of many manufacturers, wholesalers, and retailers. These two seasons are *O-Chugen* (oh-chuu-gen) in midsummer and *O-Seibo* (oh-say-boe) in early December.

Giving the right gifts to the right people during these two periods is an important social obligation in Japan. Because the know-how of seasonal gift-giving (and gift etiquette at weddings and funerals) is no longer automatically transmitted from parents to offspring, guidebooks on these subjects are perennial bestsellers.

Originally, midsummer gifts were given during the ancient festival *O-Bon* (oh-bone), or Festival of the Dead, in remembrance of those who had died during the preceding year. Also known as the Lantern Festival, on this day family members clean the tombs of those who have died and symbolically invite their spirits to return home, where they are honored with special foods. In earlier times actual lanterns were used to guide the spirits back to their former homes.

Nowadays, midyear gifts might be classified as "good relations" gifts, while those given at the end of the year are regarded as "appreciation" gifts—for favors, business, loyalty, and the like.

Beginning in the 1970s, Valentine's Day quickly developed into a major occasion, a development that some cynics accused the chocolate industry of masterminding. Valentine's Day in Japan, however, comes with a twist—women give boxes of chocolates to men, not the other way around.

Birthdays, graduations, vacation travel, and other auspicious events are also established occasions for gift giving, as are weddings, when all guests give and receive gifts. Authorities, celebrities, and individuals interviewed by the news media regularly receive gifts or cash. It is also still common to give gifts to people who provide information, advice, or offer other assistance.

As in the United States and elsewhere, gift cards are often given as gifts in Japan. The variety of gifts is now virtually unlimited, but there are certain gifts that are appropriate for specific occasions and not for others. Here are some of the regular gift-giving occasions and their appropriate gifts:

BEREAVEMENT
Money, incense, flowers, fruit, and other food items.

BIRTHDAYS
Money, clothing, accessories, candy, sports equipment, DVDs, CDs, and so on.

People's 60th, 70th, 78th, 88th, and 99th birthdays are special occasions in Japan and are marked by special parties and elaborate gifts.

SUMMER GIFT-GIVING SEASON (*O-Chugen* / oh-chuu-gane)
Alcoholic drinks, fruit packages, coffee, candy, cooking oils, and dried sheets of processed seaweed that are used in various Japanese dishes.

GET-WELL GIFTS
Money, fruit, other foods, flowers.

Visiting someone who is sick or has been in an accident is an institutionalized custom called *o-mimai* (oh-me-my). It should be noted that a potted plant is often not a welcome gift. A common superstition says that the roots of the plant symbolize a long hospital stay—literally being "rooted" in bed.

GRADUATIONS
Apparel, personal accessories, travel accessories, gift certificates, money.

YEAR-END GIFT-GIVING SEASON (*O-Seibō* / oh-say-bohh)
Beer, wine, whiskey, bulk food items, calendars.

PROMOTIONS
Personal accessories, wine, whiskey, sports equipment.

SEVEN-FIVE-THREE FESTIVAL (*Shichi-Go-San Matsuri* / she-chee-go-sahn mot-sue-ree)
Shichi-go-san (which means 7, 5, 3) is a festival celebrated by parents on the 15th of November to mark the growth of their children as they turn three, five, and seven. It dates back some 1,500 years.

At the age of seven young girls celebrate by wearing their first obi with their kimono, while at the age of five boys celebrate by wearing their first *hakama* (hah-kah-mah) trousers. Three is the traditional age when girls were allowed to let their hair grow long and boys received their first "samurai" haircut. (Nowadays, hairstyle is an individual preference, typically depending on what is in vogue among popular entertainers and television stars.) Although some parents now dress their children in formal Western attire for this event, they are more traditionally dressed in their finest Japanese garb, providing an opportunity for families, friends, and even tourists to use their cameras. Money, apparel, toys, and recreational equipment are the usual gifts.

TRAVEL
When Japanese people travel, especially abroad, they customarily bring a supply of small gifts called *o-tsukai mono* (oh-t'sue-kye moe-no), or "things to be used," to give to people they meet—particularly those who do them favors. These gifts range from hand towels, Japanese paper, fans, and scarves to inexpensive calculators.

While traveling, people almost always buy famous local products or specialty products to give to family members, friends, and professional colleagues upon their return. These gifts are called *o-miyage* (oh-mee-yah-gay).

VISITING PRIVATE HOMES
Fruit, cake, cookies, seaweed, candy, coffee, and other food items. Wines and whiskies are always in order for men. In earlier times it was not considered appropriate to give spirits to women as gifts, but many women today pride themselves on their knowledge of wines and drink them regularly. If you know a woman drinks wine—and which brand she likes—it is an especially appropriate gift.

WEDDINGS
Money is the most common gift for weddings. It is invariably presented in the form of crisp, new 10,000-yen notes in a special money envelope called a *noshibukuro* (no-she-buu-kuu-roh), sold at stationers. The minimum amount to give for the wedding of a casual acquaintance is 10,000 yen (or about US$100 at the present exchange rate).

As mentioned earlier, gift-wrapping is a special art in Japan. Customarily, gifts are wrapped in two sheets of white handmade paper and tied with special cords, or *mizuhiki* (me-zuu-hee-kee), made of rolled paper. Black-and-white cords are reserved for bereavement gifts; red, silver, and gold cords for happy occasions. Weddings and deaths call for the cords to be tied in square knots, representing permanence. Bows are acceptable on other occasions.

Naturally, there is a correct Japanese way to fold wrapping paper around a package. When the gift is for a happy event, the right side of the paper goes over the left side. When the gift is an expression of sadness, the wrapping is reversed.

Foreign visitors and residents in Japan are not expected to follow precisely Japanese protocol in wrapping gifts, but failure to give a gift on a gift-giving occasion may be regarded as insensitivity to Japanese customs.

Gift wrapping need pose no problem, however, as most stores will provide the proper wrapping at the sales counter upon request. Gifts are wrapped in paper decorated with the store's logo, but unlike in the West, such paper is totally acceptable and even preferable when the store is one that is well known and respected.

The volume of gifts received by Japanese has become so great that many gifts go unused. Companies have been set up specifically to buy unopened, unwanted gifts (at a fraction of their original cost). These companies sell the unused gifts at substantial discounts.

19

Japan's Home-Visiting Etiquette

Traditionally the Japanese did not have an established custom of inviting friends to their homes because their homes were generally small, crowded, and considered inappropriate venues for entertaining. Instead, it became the practice to invite people to public drinking places and restaurants—which is one of the reasons Japan has more restaurants and bars per capita than any other nation.

Prior to modern times it was, in fact, more likely that the Japanese would invite foreign friends to their homes rather than other Japanese people. It is still unusual for the average Japanese, particularly older people, to invite longtime friends, much less casual acquaintances, to their homes. However, with growing Westernization, affluence, and the construction of larger homes and apartments that are all or mostly Western style, such invitations have become more common.

Once you are inside the home, etiquette remains essentially the same whether the home is Western-style or Japanese-style, although in a Japanese-style room one sits on *tatami* (tah-tah-me) reed-mat flooring and food or refreshments are served on a low table.

Should you be invited to a traditional Japanese-style home, you may find that the front sliding door of the house is usually not locked and that there may not be an outside doorbell. The proper etiquette is to open the door and enter (some old homes have bells attached to the doors that will ring when they are opened). You will then be standing in a small, ground-level vestibule called the *genkan* (gane-kahn).

Once inside the *genkan* the custom is to call out *Gomen kudasai!* (Go-mane kuu-dah-sigh)—which more or less means "Excuse me!"—to announce your presence.

If you expect to be invited in, and you are wearing a rain-coat or overcoat (or hat and gloves), remove them before the host arrives to welcome you. There will be a place in the *genkan* for umbrellas, and sometimes hooks for coats. If there are no hooks, hand your coat to the host if he or she offers to take it, or carry it with you when you are invited in.

If you carry your coat into the guest or living room, the common procedure is to fold it and place it on the floor next to the wall behind you (you will normally sit around a table placed in the center of the room).

The first level of the house will usually be about six to twelve inches above the level of the *genkan*. Remove your street shoes before stepping up onto the main level. Your host will invariably place a pair of hallway slippers on the floor in front of you.

The trick is to get your shoes off without falling down or having to sit down, and to step directly from your shoes onto the main level. (When Japanese houses were originally designed, people did not wear lace-up shoes; they wore thong sandals or wooden clogs.)

The Japanese themselves simply prize their feet out of their shoes without bothering to unlace them, and then use long-handled shoe-spoons to wedge their feet back into their shoes when preparing to leave. This works fairly well if your shoes are not too tightly laced. But if you prefer to sit down on the edge of the *genkan* and take your shoes off, don't hesitate to do so.

After you are up on the wooden landing, step into the slippers and follow your host. The slippers are not worn into rooms that have reed-mat floors. They are for wooden floors only and are left in the hallway when you enter a room. (A semi-Western house may have a Western-style sitting room with a wooden floor or a carpet over it. In this case the host will expect you to keep the slippers on.)

In a typical Japanese-style *tatami* room you will be provided with a *zabuton* (zah-buu-tone), or floor cushion, to sit on.

The old Japanese way of sitting, on closed, folded legs, has long since disappeared except among geisha, those performing the tea ceremony, and people involved with other special occasions. Men generally sit cross-legged; women sit with their legs and feet pulled up on one side or the other.

Seating etiquette invariably comes into play when you are invited into a Japanese-style living room. The focal point of the room is the traditional alcove, or *tokonoma* (toe-koe-no-mah), in one corner, usually away from the door. The seat of honor is the one nearest the *tokonoma*. It is not polite to take this seat without being asked to do so, and it is good manners to decline at least once when you are directed to it.

Another point of etiquette is that the *tokonoma*, which serves as a kind of "altar" of the home, should not be used as a catchall place to put things, such as coats, packages, or trash.

Once you are seated, your host will soon serve you some kind of drink—tea, coffee, beer, or a soft drink—and usually a small snack, such as pastries, fruit, or chips. Most Japanese who host foreign visitors in their homes for meals make a point of finding out in advance what kind of Japanese food their guests prefer.

If during winter you are invited to visit a very old traditional Japanese home that does not have modern heating, you may be invited to sit around a *kotatsu* (koe-taht-sue), a quilt-covered table warmed by an electric heater (formerly burning charcoal in a brazier). With your legs extending under the *kotatsu* and the quilt covering you up to your waist, at least the lower half of your body will be kept quite warm.

Most of the advice in this chapter is also appropriate for those visiting Western-style homes in Japan. For example, even Japanese who live in totally Western-style apartments or homes do not wear their street shoes inside. All such homes are designed with a small-to-large *genkan* area where the shoes are taken off. This is generally little more than space inside the front door that has been designated as the *genkan*.

Home-visiting etiquette in Japan is basically the same as in the United States and European countries. You should simply be courteous and polite, and follow the requests or directions of your host about where to sit, and so on.

The one exception is the custom of bringing a host or hostess gifts—most often pastries, fruit, cookies, or candy, and sometimes whiskey, sake, or wine—a custom that is more strictly observed in Japan than in the United States.

20

Tea Ceremony Protocol

Foreigners in Japan who are invited to attend a tea ceremony performed by a skilled tea master are fortunate indeed. The tea ceremony, or *chanoyu* (chah-no-you), combines Japan's ancient systems of aesthetics and etiquette in one setting—one ceremony that attempts to say it all.

The tea ceremony is therefore many elements in one. It is a display of aestheticism and order, an exercise in control of the mind and body, an attempt to attain the ideal interpersonal relationship and harmony with the cosmos, and in sum, an opportunity to enjoy a very sensual, highly refined style of living.

Japan's Emperor Shomu, who reigned from 724 to 749, is credited with introducing tea in Japan after he was presented with some bricks of pressed tea leaves by a famous Chinese priest named Ganjin. Soon after being introduced to the delightful custom of drinking tea, the emperor made a practice of inviting people to join him. He once invited one hundred Buddhist monks to his palace for a tea party.

During the Heian period (794–1185), a tea made of steamed and dried tea leaves ground into a powder became popular. Called *matcha* (maht-chah), this is the tea still used today in the tea ceremony. But it was not until the fifteenth century that the tea ceremony, under the patronage of Shogun Yoshimasa Ashikaga (1436–1490), became a full-fledged aesthetic, philosophical, and spiritual ritual.

Japanese authorities credit Juko Murata, tea master to Ashikaga, with adding the artistic and spiritual dimension that was incorporated into *Sado* (sah-doe), or "The Way of Tea," in the late 1400s. He is also credited with originating the practice of holding the tea ceremony in a special house or room.

Murata introduced the concepts of *wabi* (wah-bee), *sabi* (sah-bee), and *yugen* (yuu-gen) into the tea ceremony. *Wabi* refers to a richness, fullness, and serenity found in simplicity. *Sabi* refers to solitude, quiet grandeur, age, and naturalness. *Yugen* is the mysterious, tranquil beauty that exists just below the surface of a thing. Murata's philosophy of *chanoyu* was heavily tinged with pathos and the transience of all things.

About a century later, Sen no Rikyu, an ethnic-Korean Osaka merchant turned tea master, put even more emphasis on the Zen Buddhist concepts of simplicity, spiritual tranquility, and communion with nature in his tea ceremonies, reportedly as a way of countering the snobbery and pretension that existed among his fellow merchants. He also introduced the idea of using a simple but carefully designed and furnished rustic tea "hut" that measured only about twelve by thirteen feet and was separate from the pavilion or room where the guests gathered and waited for the ceremony to begin.

Rikyu further formalized the tea ceremony by establishing rules applying to the attitude and responsibility of the tea host. Some of these were: make sure your guests feel warm in winter and cool in summer; arrange the flowers so they look like wildflowers; make sure the charcoal is properly prepared so the hot water will be just right for the tea;

be quick and efficient; be prepared for rain even on a clear day; be attentive toward all of the guests; serve the tea with insight into the spirits of your guests.

After attracting the attention of the powerful warlord Hideyoshi Toyotomi, who had become shogun, Rikyu was designated as his tea master. Some time later the warlord demanded Rikyu's daughter as a concubine. The tea master refused. In 1591 the despot ordered the master to commit suicide, which he did after a farewell tea ceremony.

The *suki-ya* (ski-yah), or teahouse, that came into use after Juko Murata and Sen no Rikyu accommodated a maximum of five people. It also had a service room where the utensils were washed and readied. The room had two entrances—one for the host and the other for guests. The doorway for guests was very low, requiring that they enter the room on their hands and knees to humble themselves in preparation for the ceremony—another of Rikyu's ideas.

Present-day teahouses vary in size and degree of luxury but the basic design has remained the same. Several tea ceremony schools have emerged, each with its own style. Some are very formal; others are informal and include a full meal made up of a number of small dishes that originated in Buddhist temples. Some groups hold their ceremonies outside. The three leading schools are Ura-senke, Omote-senke, and Mushakoji. The first two of these schools were founded by competing members of the same family, resulting in one of them setting up his school in the *omote* or front of the house and the other one conducting his school in the *ura* or rear of the house.

While a tea ceremony can be held at any time on any occasion, there are several traditional times with different forms. *Akatsuki no chanoyu* (ah-kaht-ski no chah-no-you), or "sunrise tea ceremony," begins around 3:00 AM, when the moon is still bright in the sky, and ends by 6:00 AM.

Asa no chanoyu (ah-sah no chah-no-you), or "morning tea ceremony," begins around 6:00 and is popular in the summer months when it is still cool early in the morning.

Shogo no saji (show-go no sah-jee), or "noon tea," begins at noon and lasts for three or more hours.

Yoban-ashi no chanoyu (yoh-bahn-ah-she no chah-no-yuu), or "leisurely evening tea ceremony," usually begins around 6:00 PM and lasts as long as the guests want to stay.

Finally, there is the *rinji chanoyu* (reen-jee chah-no-yuu), or "special tea ceremony," which is usually held on short notice to mark the visit of a special friend or guest or to celebrate an especially beautiful time of the year, such as when the cherry trees are blooming or when there has been a heavy snowfall.

It should be noted that some kind of light food is served at virtually all tea ceremonies to prepare the stomach for the tea, which is very strong (and possibly unpalatable to those not accustomed to it).

Several tea-ceremony schools and organizations offer ceremonies that are designed to attract large numbers of people. These ceremonies tend to be commercialized, with the operation of a profitable business being the primary aim. Very little of the deeper meaning of the traditional ceremony comes through at these sessions.

A deeply traditional tea ceremony begins when a host invites guests and starts preparing for the ceremony, usually a number of days in advance. The site for the ceremony should always be a quiet place where interruptions are unlikely. On the day of the ceremony, the host carefully sweeps and waters down the outside area, then cleans the tearoom and utensils and prepares any special dishes to be served.

The host generally greets the guests in the waiting room and then withdraws. Purists among the guests will change into clean socks before entering the tearoom.

At the designated time, which may be announced by the sounding of a gong, the guests leave all their belongings in the waiting room, wash their hands in a bowl provided for that purpose outside of the tearoom, and crawl into the room, leaving their shoes outside. They may enter the room in the order of seniority, determined by age, experience, or relationship to the tea master.

After entering the tearoom each guest turns around and moves his or her shoes out of the way, arranging them neatly and pointed outward. Each guest then slowly and methodically goes to the *tokonoma* (toe-koe-no-mah), or alcove, to admire the hanging scroll there. After all have entered the room and admired the *tokonoma* display, they seat themselves before the brazier in order of seniority.

Conversation and comments are subdued and thoughtful, in keeping with the surroundings and purpose of the ceremony. The host enters and formally welcomes each guest, bowing to each of them. The guests return the bows. The host then lights incense sticks. Guests may inspect the incense box to admire its beauty.

If food is to be included in the ceremony it is served at this time. Guests inspect the food and serving ware carefully and eat slowly, savoring the experience. When the meal is finished, the guests return to the waiting room while the host cleans the tearoom, exchanges the alcove scroll for a flower arrangement, and brings out the utensils to be used in the tea ceremony.

When these preparations are completed the guests are called in again. They admire the flower arrangement and the tea utensils before seating themselves. The host returns, ceremoniously prepares the tea, and then begins the service by passing the large tea bowl to the highest ranking guest.

The guest holds the tea bowl in his or her left hand, turns it twice clockwise with the right hand so the motif on the bowl faces the host, takes three and a half sips, sets the bowl down, wipes the edge of the bowl where he or she drank with a cloth, rotates the bowl again so the motif is facing him or her, and then passes it to the next guest.

After each guest has repeated this ceremony the tea bowl is passed back to the host, who cleans it and hands it back to the guests to examine and admire. Bowls and other utensils used in the traditional ceremony are usually masterpieces of craftsmanship, often hundreds of years old, and are representative of what the Japanese call *shibui* (she-buu-ee) beauty—the epitome of simplicity, naturalness, and harmony.

All the other utensils used in the ceremony are again examined and discussed, each guest striving to merge with the spirit of the object. Afterward, the host may serve something sweet, accompanied by ordinary tea, either green or black, in individual teacups.

This part of the ceremony is more casual, but still carefully orchestrated. At the appropriate time, the senior guest takes the lead in bowing to the host and thanking him or her for the ceremony. The other guests follow suit, and all leave.

The dedicated host may then prepare a final cup of tea, and in silence and solitude, sip it slowly, savoring the atmosphere to the fullest.

Newcomers to the tea ceremony may question other guests on points of behavior before the ceremony begins, and should follow their lead during the ceremony. Each of the commercial *chanoyu* schools has its own literature describing its ceremony. If you attend a ceremony open to the public you will most likely receive a small printed guide on what to do during the ceremony.

Traditionally, friends and others were invited to tea ceremonies as guests of the tea master who prepared the tea and served them. This is still the norm, but there are now public demonstrations where visitors are invited to either view the ceremony without taking part in it, or actually perform the ceremony themselves.

If you are scheduled to perform a ceremony you will first observe how the tea master conducts a ceremony. When it is your turn you will be guided through the steps by the tea master.

At all times during a tea ceremony the rule is to be as quiet and as tranquil as possible, totally at peace with yourself and the world.

21

Japan's Festival Culture

Some of the most impressive historical legacies that have been kept alive in Japan are *matsuri* (mot-sue-ree), or "festivals." Virtually every village, town, and city, as well as thousands of temples and shrines throughout the country, celebrate one or more annual festivals.

Visitors who would like to see and experience one of the most interesting facets of Japanese life should take in a shrine or temple festival if the opportunity arises. Festival calendars are widely available at tourist information centers, travel agencies, and hotel concierge desks.

A limited calendar of the celebrations considered to be of special interest to foreign visitors includes a total of 271 *matsuri*. Travel books in English generally list only a very small number of these events—often the "big eight" or "big ten" festivals that take place in the largest cities and are seen as national events.

There are, in fact, thirteen festivals in Japan that are national holidays, some of which last for several days. *Shogatsu* (Show-got-sue) or New Year's, begins on the eve of December 31 and ends on January 7, although many workers take additional days off.

The reason for the number and variety of *matsuri* in Japan can be traced to Shinto, which holds that all things in nature—trees, rocks, mountains, water, and so on—have spirits, and that people must remain on good terms with these spirits to prevent evil and destructive things from happening. Until the last decades of the nineteenth century, Japan's economy was based on agriculture and depended on the success of seasonal harvests—and, therefore, on the cooperation of these natural spirits. Religious rituals became important traditions year round to ensure the spirits' goodwill, inviting the appropriate deities to come down from heaven so the people could pray to them directly.

Matsuri to help ward off diseases and other calamities also became common. Some festivals were meant to ensure fertility; other festivals were designed to bring peace to the spirits of physical things—including broken and discarded sewing needles, harkening back to the time when most people made their own clothes.

Paper lanterns, huge drums, gongs, masks, dolls, and historical images are fundamental parts of many Japanese festivals, as are fireworks.

In keeping with the Japanese love of structure and organization, the *matsuri* were (and are) made up of three parts. The first part is called *kami mukae* (kah-me muu-kigh), or "meeting the gods"; it is a ceremony held at a shrine or other sacred place to welcome the gods to the Earth. The deity concerned descends from heaven and takes up temporary residence in a palanquin-like portable shrine called a *mikoshi* (me-koh-she).

The second part of a festival, called *shinkoh* (sheen-koh), consists of participants carrying the *mikoshi* around rural communities and through the streets of towns and cities, generally accompanied by chants and some kind of music.

The third part of a *matsuri* is the *kami okuri* (kah-me oh-kuu-ree), or "god send-off," a ritual to send the god concerned back to heaven.

Among the most popular of Japan's annual festivals are the *odori matsuri* (oh-doh-ree mot-sue-ree) or dance festivals, in which participants wearing colorful yukata robes and traditional sedge hats dance through the streets.

Kyoto is especially famous for its festivals, some of which date back to the eighth and ninth centuries and go on for days. Named for a Kyoto district famous for its geisha houses, *Gion Matsuri* (Ghee-own Mot-sue-ree) is staged by the Yasaka Shrine. It begins on July 1 each year and lasts until the 29th. The biggest *Gion* events occur on July 16 and 17. Kyoto's biggest fall festival is the *Jidai Matsuri* (Jee-die Mot-sue-re), which means "Festival of the Ages." It occurs in the latter part of October, and during its celebration participants dress in the styles of various periods of Japan's history, from the nineteenth century all the way back to the eighth century, with some 1,700 marchers divided into 20 groups.

Japan has a number of curious festivals that attract large audiences. Among them: mud-slinging, paying homage to phallic images, eating and drinking from huge bowls, viewing parades by jokers and clowns, and *matsuri* in which the participants laugh and laugh until they are free from all stress and bad feelings.

Among Japan's dozens of annual celebrations and hundreds of festivals, the celebration of the New Year stands out as one of the most important. As mentioned earlier, this is known as *Shogatsu* and includes the celebration of New Year's Eve, New Year's Day, and the first few days of January. In addition to *Omisoka* (Oh-me-soh-kah), or New Year's Eve, there are two major celebrations associated with *Shogatsu:* *Joya no Kane* (Joh-yah no Kah-nay), or "Ringing in the New Year," and *Hatsumode* (Hot-sue-moh-day), or "First Visit."

On New Year's Eve crowds make their way to temples that have huge bells for the celebration of *Joya no Kane*. As midnight approaches, gangs of young men dressed in traditional loincloths (despite the frigid temperatures in the central and northern parts of the islands) take turns swinging large log clappers against the bells a total of 108 times, representing the 108 sins that according to Buddhism afflict mankind. Each time the temple bell is rung one of these sins is eliminated. Great effort is made to time the last of the 108 rings with the stroke of midnight, thereby allowing everyone to begin the new year with a clean slate.

This annual ritual has been practiced for centuries, but has nonetheless changed in the modern world: A number of the more famous shrines and temples around the country televise their celebration of *Joya no Kane*. These broadcasts are viewed by millions of people in their homes and in public places. At the stroke of midnight, those in pubs and other such places mark the end of *Omisoka* and the beginning of the new year with shouts and toasts.

Hatsumode, the second major New Year's ritual, is the age-old custom of going to a shrine or temple between midnight on New Year's Eve and January 7 to pray for health and happiness during the coming year. Huge numbers of people, including many resident and foreign visitors, begin heading toward shrines or temples sometime before midnight, with the intention of reaching their destinations just before or precisely at 12 AM.

In Tokyo, hundreds of thousands of people celebrate *Hatsumode* at the famous Meiji Shrine, which is located in a wooded park adjoining Harajuku station on the city's Yamanote loop line. Thousands of people arrive in Harajuku via the Yamanote train line, while others arrive at the adjoining Meji Jingumae station via the Chiyoda line.

But many, many thousands of subway commuters prefer to disembark at Omotesando Station (the station just before Meiji Jingumae) and walk down the wide Omotesando Boulevard to the entrance to the shrine grounds. This is the approach that I recommend visitors take, walking in the company of good friends to fully enjoy the experience. (One thing to keep in mind is that New Year's Eve in Tokyo can be very cold; plan ahead and wear warm clothing.)

Even if they can't go on New Year's Eve, travelers in Japan should make a point of visiting a shrine or temple on one of the first few days of the New Year. During this time the whole of Japan has a festive look and feel, and you can visit street stalls galore and see children and young women dressed in colorful kimono.

The huge Sensoji Shrine complex in Tokyo's Asakusa Ward is one of the city's most popular locations for *Hatsumode*. It is located on the northeastern end of the Ginza subway line, about a 20-minute ride from central Tokyo. The long mall leading to the shrine is flanked by one hundred or more retail stalls.

Visitors are welcome at all of Japan's festivals. In some cases, such as the famous *odori matsuri*, you may even join in if you wish (after borrowing or buying the traditional yukata costume to wear).

22

The Importance of the Apology

The Japanese are famous for apologizing. They apologize often and in a wide variety of situations. Indeed, *sumi-masen* (sue-me-mah-sen), the word most commonly used for "Excuse me" or "I'm sorry," is also used to say "Thank you." (Note that in everyday use the *U* in this word isn't enunciated clearly, making it sound like "see-mah-sin".)

The subtleties of this overlapping usage go to the heart of traditional Japanese culture, which, as mentioned earlier, was based on the concept of *wa* (wah), or harmony. An overwhelming need for harmony led the Japanese to express themselves in highly stylized and ambiguous ways that were calculated not to give offense. But even when speaking in an esoteric, poetic, and indirect manner, there was still always the danger of rubbing someone the wrong way, so apologizing in advance became a standard practice during and after almost every conversation.

On any given day when out and about in Japan, one can hear dozens of verbal apologies. Many of them may sound silly or inappropriate to the outsider, but they are an institutionalized element in Japanese interaction.

Following the prescribed forms of physical etiquette was vital in feudal Japan—from bowing to parents, teachers, or others in authority, to moving off a road and kowtowing when a clan lord and his procession passed. But adhering to the demanding verbal etiquette was even more critical.

In this society where the slightest deviation from the highest standards of behavior could be a serious transgression, it was essential to have a socially accepted mechanism to atone for real as well as imaginary slights. This mechanism was the apology, and it could take a variety of forms, ranging from suicide by a ritualistic slicing open of the abdomen to simply saying *sumimasen.* Verbal apologies as well as some of the more drastic forms of apology are still distinctive aspects of contemporary Japanese life.

The power of the apology is also important in the public realm. Politicians and businessmen whose behavior has "insulted" the public routinely resign as a form of apology. This action, however, has lost a great deal of its impact because of an increase in the number of scandals that have resulted in the resignations of scores of top business and political leaders.

It is essential that foreign visitors in Japan be aware of the power of the apology. As with any deviation from social norms, Japanese people can be highly sensitive to a failure to apologize on any of the numerous daily occasions when an apology is appropriate or expected. While the Japanese generally accept that foreigners can't be expected to follow Japanese apology etiquette, they often can't prevent themselves from reacting emotionally when such breaches occur. This emotionalism colors their opinions of foreigners and their reactions to them.

If you are not thoroughly familiar with Japanese language or culture, the best procedure is to use the expression *sumimasen* whenever you feel an apology might be called for. If an apology was not called for, the Japanese will just think you are exceptionally polite—a character trait they appreciate and constantly cultivate themselves.

Another common expression of apology is *gomen nasai* (go-mane nah-sie). This term is stronger than *sumimasen* and used in more serious situations, when the connotation is closer to "I'm sorry" than "Excuse me."

23

Expressing Appreciation

Expressing and demonstrating appreciation has traditionally been an integral part of the Japanese etiquette system. As with other elements of that system, however, its
rules and prescriptions were carried far beyond the norms
of accepted behavior in the West. In the Japanese system
every action required a balancing reaction, as in the Chinese
principle of *yin* and *yang*, in which opposing forces balance
and bring about harmony.

Appreciation was the expected response for any favor,
assistance, or positive recognition; it was also required for
repaying debts that came to one naturally as a result of
birth—debts to one's parents, to instructors, to the clan lord,
to the emperor, to the gods.

Verbal expressions of appreciation and "thank you" bows
were as common as expressions of apology (if not more common). Again, the golden rule was to maintain harmony at all
levels by sustaining maximum goodwill and emotional satisfaction. Verbal expressions of appreciation were generally
accompanied by bows, ranging from very light to medium,
depending on the circumstances. The more important the
situation the more formal and deeper the required bow.

In addition to *sumimasen,* other Japanese terms for "thank you" include, in order of politeness: *Domo arigato gozaimasu* (doe-moe ah-ree-gah-toe go-zye-mahss), *Arigato gozaimasu* (ah-ree-gah-toe go-zye-mahss), and *Domo* (doe-moe). These are among the most common words you will hear in Japan.

It is customary to thank people twice for treating you to drinks or food—first when they treat you, and again the next time you see them (if no more than two or three weeks have elapsed). At this subsequent meeting, the institutionalized phrase to use is *Kono aida, domo arigato gozaimasu* (koe-no-aye-dah doe-moe ah-ree-gah-toe go-zie-mahss), which means "Thank you very much for the other day" (or "not long ago" or "recently").

Verbal expressions of appreciation, however, are too ephemeral (not to mention potentially insincere) to give the emotional satisfaction required to maintain harmony. Institutionalized gift giving is a logical response to this need for more meaningful ways of demonstrating appreciation.

In today's Japan, all the traditional ways of expressing and demonstrating appreciation continue to flourish. The Japanese not only give gifts in appreciation of past favors and goodwill, but also as payment in advance for future goodwill and favors.

This often strikes Westerners as bribery and therefore unethical behavior. A careful analysis of this system reveals, however, an intimate understanding of human nature and a degree of common sense at work that may attain better and even fairer results than the "ethically" based Western approach. For example, in the past people who planned to entertain guests at a restaurant would customarily tip the employees a day or so in advance to make sure they got the best possible reception and service.

Emulation of the Japanese custom of expressing and demonstrating appreciation before and after a favor is granted will allow the outsider to function more smoothly and effectively in the Japanese environment.

One challenge for foreign visitors is being aware of the special occasions when something more than casual verbal thanks is required. For businesspeople, one of the most important of these special occasions is at the beginning of the New Year. Between January third and the tenth or eleventh, most professionals personally visit as many of their customers and suppliers as they can, thanking them for past patronage and asking them to continue doing business with them during the New Year. This custom is known as *aisatsu mawari* (aye-sot-sue mah-wah-ree), or "round of greetings."

Following the lead of the Japanese themselves, foreign visitors to Japan expecting to meet people outside of the travel industry should take along small courtesy gifts to hand out to anyone who befriends them. If you are going to meet people with whom you hope to develop long-term relationships, gifts more appropriate for the situation and rank of the individuals involved may be advisable.

24

Dating in Japan

In historical terms the concept of dating is still quite new in Japan. Dating as it is practiced in the West did not appear in Japan until the middle of the 1950s. In feudal Japan the custom was to separate boys and girls at a fairly early age for education and training, and thereafter strictly limit social relations among teenagers of the opposite sex.

Virtually all marriages were arranged. Love, when it occurred, was looked upon as forbidden fruit and disruptive of the social order. Although it may sound odd, true love relationships were more likely to occur between customers and women working as prostitutes in the inns and red-light districts that dotted the country. Such an environment was really the only one in which a couple could be, if only temporarily, free from social constraints. (After the shogunate period ended in the late 1860s, it was fairly common for men of high rank to marry their geisha lovers—one such individual going on to become the prime minister.)

Relatively recent historical events set the stage for the development of personal relations that would lead to dating and love marriages. The introduction of democracy in Japan in 1946 allowed new individual freedoms, as did the end of the feudal family system in which the father held absolute sway over the members of his family. The young Japanese of this era gradually began picking up the dating custom from the hundreds of thousands of American and Allied soldiers serving in the military forces that occupied Japan from 1945 to 1952.

It wasn't until well into the 1950s, however, that dating started to become a significant part of the Japanese experience. Single Japanese felt free enough to express themselves individually and were affluent enough to spend money purely for entertainment.

Age-old customs and attitudes continued to maintain sharp divisions between the adult male and female worlds in Japan, preventing large numbers of people from establishing personal relationships with the opposite sex that led to marriage. As a result, somewhere between 10 and 20 percent of young Japanese men and women still do not date—most saying they don't have time to develop the necessary relationships—and depend on third parties to arrange marriages for them.

Other eligible singles in Japan meet much as they do in the West. Popular meeting places include schools, restaurants, pubs, swimming pools, tennis courts, beaches, mountains, and so on. Many dating couples in Japan are also brought together by professional online dating bureaus and by superiors at the workplace.

Except among very internationalized families, boys and young men generally do not go to the homes of their girlfriends to pick them up or socialize—or take them home when the date ends. Instead, they rendezvous at train stations, coffee shops, restaurants, and other public places.

Dating couples in Japan engage in the same activities that couples do in the West—going to restaurants, night spots, theaters, beaches, and mountains; taking weekend drives; and so on. At the same time, public displays of affection remain significantly more restrained than the West.

Most Japanese apartments and homes are not large enough or private enough to serve as trysting places for lovers. For this reason, a large national network of small hotels and inns, known as "love hotels," has arisen to cater to Japanese couples seeking privacy.

Today dating has become relatively internationalized in Japan. Interracial and multi-ethnic couples—either dating or married—are now common enough that they are no longer subject to being stared at.

Historically, however, the Japanese attitude toward interracial couples was strongly negative. Traditional Japanese culture was so group-oriented and so exclusive that it was difficult for any group to accept an outsider into the fold— even if the person was Japanese. Accepting a non-Japanese was practically unthinkable.

Some Japanese, like their Western counterparts, have not accepted interracial dating or interracial marriages as natural or desirable, and remain opposed to them. Nonetheless, tolerance of these liaisons is growing among the Japanese majority. An increasing number of internationalized Japanese parents even see interracial dating and marriages as highly desirable—as one of the avenues by which the Japanese can become truly international. These people are delighted when their sons and daughters marry economically and socially acceptable non-Japanese.

Due to the more relaxed attitude concerning interracial liaisons, some foreigners in Japan may find engaging in interracial relationships is easier than it would be in their home countries.

Given the still-acute sensitivity of the average Japanese, foreign visitors and residents are advised to behave in a conservative manner and avoid conspicuously aggressive over-tures to members of the opposite sex in public.

The overriding rule of dating etiquette in Japan is to fol-low the Japanese pattern of behavior and not engage in con-duct that could be regarded as rude or unacceptable in any country.

25

Wedding Customs

Most weddings in Japan consist of Shinto, Buddhist, or Christian ceremonies. The most popular is a western-style "white wedding," which is now chosen by most young couples. These wedding are held in a church, or more commonly a wedding hall or hotel chapel, and are frequently administered by an unordained westerner who acts the role of a minister.

The most traditional wedding is the Shinto ceremony. It became especially popular after Emperor Taisho was wedded in this type of ceremony in 1900.

The actual Shinto wedding ceremony, which is generally attended only by the families and close friends of the couple, is simple and lasts about 20 to 30 minutes. A Shinto priest consecrates the union. Usually the bride and groom enter the ceremonial hall preceded by a Shinto shrine maiden. Behind them are the go-between and his or her spouse, followed by the groom's parents and immediate family, and the bride's parents and immediate family.

The go-between, or *nakodo* (nah-koe-doe), traditionally was the one who made the match between the young couple. Today, with arranged marriages becoming less and less common, the person who takes this part in the wedding is more like a best man, as in the West.

In a pure Shinto ceremony both the bride and groom usually wear traditional wedding kimono. The bride wears an elaborate wig called a *takashimada* (tah-kah-she-mah-dah) and a white headdress called a *tsuno-kakushi* (t'sue-no-kah-koo-she), literally, "horn hider"—a name that comes from the ancient belief that jealousy could turn women into angry demons with horns. This headdress served as a warning that it was best to "hide one's horns."

After the priest announces the union, all stand and bow. Then the *sansankudo* (san-san-kuu-doe) ceremony is performed. This consists of the bride and groom each taking three sips of sake from three different-sized cups that symbolize their union. The couple then reads wedding vows from a scroll. An exchange of wedding rings may or may not follow, depending on the couple's wishes.

Finally, a branch of the sacred *sakaki* (sah-kah-kee) tree is offered to the gods, and the bride's and groom's families each sip a cup of sake, drinking it dry in three sips. This symbolizes the union of the families and marks the end of the ceremony.

Although Shinto wedding ceremonies are common, some Japanese people prefer Buddhist or Christian ceremonies, or numerous variations of other traditional wedding rites. I attended one rather unusual Shinto wedding in which the bride wore a kimono and the groom a tuxedo. The couple marched into the hall to the refrain of "Here Comes the Bride" and cut their Western wedding cake with a samurai sword.

Receptions, unlike most actual wedding ceremonies, are large events with anywhere from fifty to several hundred guests in attendance. It is virtually mandatory that both the bride's and the groom's coworkers, including one or more of their superiors, attend the reception. Popular places for receptions include international hotels, wedding halls, and large restaurants.

An invitation to a reception will probably include a reply postcard. You should write your name and address on this and indicate whether or not you will attend. Write a short congratulatory message and, if unable to attend, a short explanation.

It is customary to bring a cash gift to the reception. Close friends, however, can also give gifts in the Western fashion, but these should be mailed early enough to arrive two weeks before the wedding. The typical cash gift is currently between 20,000 and 50,000 yen (between US$190 and US$470, at the time of this book's publication). This, of course, varies according to your relationship with the couple. It is best to ask Japanese friends for advice on how much to give for a particular wedding.

The money, in crisp new notes, should be enclosed in a special envelope called *noshibukuro* (no-she-buu-kuu-roe). These red and white envelopes, which are sold at both stationery and convenience stores, are tied with a square knot of gold and silver cords and bear the Chinese character for *kotobuki* (koe-toe-buu-kee), meaning "happiness." In one corner is a decoration called *noshi* (no-she), which gives the envelope its name. Originally this was an actual piece of dried abalone but today it is a paper decoration.

Keep in mind that the elaborateness of the envelope should correspond to the amount of money enclosed. It is bad form to buy a very fancy envelope, no matter how pretty, and then enclose a lesser amount than the envelope suggests.

Very fancy envelopes have elaborate gold and silver cords, and plum, bamboo, and pine decorations in addition to the *noshi.* These are suitable for amounts over 50,000 yen. A suitable envelope for 20,000 yen has flat gold and silver cords, a *noshi* decoration in the corner, and no extra folds or decorations.

Tables will be set up at the entrance to the reception hall and this is where you present the *noshibukuro*.

For men, the usual attire for a wedding ceremony or reception is black suit, white shirt, and white tie. Women wear either kimono or a Western-style dress. Invitations often say to dress casually, but don't take this seriously unless you want to stand out.

Usually, receptions are formal, structured affairs, with either a skilled acquaintance or a professional serving as the master of ceremonies. Receptions may take many forms, with the three most common being a sit-down meal, a Chinese-style meal with about eight guests to a round table, or a buffet-style stand-up party.

After the newlyweds arrive to loud applause and often to the strains of the "Wedding March," the master of ceremonies introduces the go-between and him- or herself. The go-between then makes a speech about the couple, which is followed by a few more speeches by family members. The first few speeches are formal and complimentary. The tone is felicitous with no off-color jokes.

Finally, everyone stands for the toast and from here on the atmosphere becomes less formal. Next may come the cutting of the wedding cake. Then dinner is served, and the bride and groom will probably make a speech. The couple will then likely change into other clothes. (They may change as many as three times before the day is done.)

Afterward, friends of both the bride and groom take turns at the microphone, relating incidents from the past. These speeches are invariably lighter in tone, and often humorous as well as a bit embarrassing to the bride or groom. Congratulatory messages may also be read at this time. (If you are called upon to give a speech, note that it is improper to include words such as *part, leave, return*, or anything relating to separation or sadness.)

Finally, one of the parents of either the bride or groom will pay his or her respects to the guests with a short speech. The bride and groom may then present their parents with bouquets. This marks the end of the reception. The newlyweds and family see the guests off at the door, where guests receive a gift, called *hikidemono* (hee-kee-day-moe-no), loosely translated as "parting gift."

26

Wakes, Funerals &
Memorial Services

Both visitors to Japan and foreign residents there may have occasion to attend a wake, funeral, or memorial service for a Japanese friend or acquaintance, and a few pointers on what to expect can be very useful.

Most such observances in Japan are conducted according to Buddhist rites that differ somewhat depending on the sect.

The first event following the death is a wake, or *tsuya* (t'sue-yah), attended by family members and close friends. These usually start at around 6 PM in the winter and 7 PM during the summer. They may continue as late as 10 PM to accommodate the flow of mourners. Incense sticks are burned and a Buddhist priest recites sutras. Mourners then take turns burning pinches of incense.

The day after the wake, the funeral service is held at the home of the deceased or at a local temple or funeral hall. In the most common Buddhist-style funerals, the altar is prepared with a tablet inscribed with the name and a picture of the deceased, candle holders, incense burners, flowers, and other Buddhist ritual implements.

Where to sit and exactly what to do at wakes, funerals, and memorials can be quite complicated for those who have never attended such events, but there are always people on hand to guide those who are unfamiliar with the procedures.

The best approach when you first arrive is to inform the host or whoever greets you that you have never attended a similar event before and ask them to tell you what to do and how to do it.

Upon arriving at the funeral site, proceed to the reception table, offer a word of condolence, and sign your name in the book provided. Then place an envelope of _kōden_ (koe-dane) or condolence money on a table prepared for that purpose. You can add a simple phrase such as _Go-reizen ni dozo_ (go-ray-zen nee doe-zoe), which roughly translates as "This is something for the departed."

The funeral rites begin with the recitation of sutras by a Buddhist priest and conclude with family members and relatives burning pinches of incense in turn while the priest continues to recite sutras. The priest and family of the deceased then move to the side of the altar to make room for other participants to come to the altar and pay their last respects by burning pinches of incense.

Condolence money brought to funerals should be enclosed in a special envelope called _busshugi-bukuro_ (boo-shuu-ghee-buu-kuu-roh) or _kōden-bukuro_ (kohh-dane-buu-kuu-roh). These are available at any stationery store and most convenience stores. The simplest method of choosing an envelope is to ask for the one marked _go-reizen_ (go-ray-zen). This means "before the spirit of the departed" and is acceptable for any religion.

Inside the outer folded paper is another envelope. This is where you put the money. The amount varies depending on your relationship to the deceased. If the deceased was someone you never met or knew only fleetingly—such as a relative of a coworker or acquaintance—5,000 yen (US$47) is usually appropriate. The minimum for a friend or business acquaintance is 10,000 yen (US$95 at the current exchange rate). Between 10,000 and 50,000 yen (US$95 and US$470) is the minimum if the deceased was a relative.

Mark the front of the inner envelope with the cash amount enclosed; write your name and address on the lower left corner of the back of the inner envelope. The name of the deceased is written down the center on the front of the outer envelope. Instructions for folding the envelope are usually included.

If you wish to offer a word of condolence to the family a good phrase to know is *Go-shusho-sama de gozaimasu* (go-shuu-shoh-sah-mah day go-zie-mahss), which is the equivalent of "You have my deepest sympathies."

Following the prayer chanting, a light meal may be served. If you were not very close to the deceased, it is customary to leave before the meal is served.

Wearing the correct attire to wakes and funerals is important. Men wear black suits, black neckties, socks, and shoes. Women wear black suits or dresses, black stockings, black shoes, and carry a black handbag. Make-up should be kept to a minimum and accessories in general are unacceptable. Anything shiny, such as patent leather or vinyl shoes or handbags, is taboo. However, wedding and engagement rings or simple pearl necklaces are permissible.

It is customary for the family of the deceased to set up a small altar in the home that will include one or more photographs of the deceased, other items pertaining to his or her life, and materials for burning incense. Only close friends of the deceased and the family are invited to home memorial services.

Those who visit the home to pay respects to the deceased proceed to the altar, kneel or sit down, bow, light an incense stick, bow again, and then move away from the altar for a brief visit with the family.

How long this home commemorative altar is kept is up to the individual family. In some cases it becomes a permanent fixture in the home.

27

Shrine & Temple Etiquette

There are thousands of Shinto shrines and Buddhist temples in Japan, some of which date back nearly 2,000 years and are famous for the roles they have played in Japanese history. Many of them are major attractions for both Japanese and foreign tourists, with more than a million visitors each year.

Buddhist temples are called *o'tera* (oh-tay-rah); Shinto shrines and are called *jinja* (jeen-jah).

The most distinguishing feature of Shinto shrines is the *torii* (toe-reee), or "gate," that stands in front of all shrines and has long been symbolic of Japan. The *torii* consists of two upright pillars with two crossbeams at the top. The primary function of the *torii* is to mark the boundary of the shrine. It also signals visitors that they are inside sacred precincts and should behave accordingly.

The larger the shrine and the shrine grounds, the larger its *torii* is. If the shrine grounds are expansive, there may be two or more of these gates over the walkways leading up to the shrine. Traditional etiquette dictated that once people passed under the first *torii* they were to remain quiet and behave in a reverent manner.

Nowadays, however, after you pass beneath the main *torii* of some shrines you will find the walkways lined with shops of all kinds, and any pretense of reverence and tranquility is gone. The rows of shops leading up to the great shine in Tokyo's Asakusa district are a perfect example of the commercial side of shrine visits.

At the entrance to a shrine you will often see a pair of "Korean dog" stone statues called *Koma-inu* (koh-mah-ee-nuu), one guarding each side of the entrance. They are slightly asymmetrical and one always has its mouth open, while the other has its mouth closed.

Toward the rear of the shrine precincts you will usually find the *haiden* (hi-dane), or main hall of worship. Near the *haiden* is a water fountain for rinsing your hands and mouth. This is a symbolic purification ritual that one is expected to perform before approaching the inner portion of the shrine.

After entering the main hall, you will see a heavy rope, under which is a wooden donation box, or *saisen-bako* (sie-sen-bah-koe). You should throw a donation into the box, then pull the rope that is attached to the eaves, where it rings a bell. This is to attract the attention of the shrine deity. You then clap your hands two or three times and bow your head, holding the bow for a few seconds.

There is also a main sanctuary, or *honden* (hone-dane), where the spirit of the shrine deity is believed to reside. Photography is usually permitted in the outer areas of shrines, but watch for signs in the *haiden* and *honden*.

Buddhist temples (*o'tera*) are generally marked by large, ornate gates that some people may think are the temples themselves. The gates are usually a short distance from the temple buildings. In front of *o'tera* there is a row of large incense burners along with stalls or windows where visitors buy bundles of incense sticks (*o'senko*/oh-sen-koh). After lighting one of these incense sticks it is customary to wave some of the smoke over yourself, since it is believed to have healing powers.

When entering temple buildings you may be required to take off your shoes, leaving them on shelves at the entrance or placing them in plastic bags and taking them with you. (Note also that Nijō Castle in Kyoto, one of the most visited historical buildings in Japan, requires visitors to remove their shoes at the entrance. Traditional castles that allow visitors to enter main buildings generally have a no-shoes policy.)

Photography is generally permitted on temple grounds, but it may be forbidden inside the various buildings. Signs are usually posted where it is prohibited.

Both Shinto shrines and Buddhist temples can range in size from a small building to a large complex that contains numerous buildings of varying sizes that are used for meetings and services. Sometimes the temples or shrines are little more than tiny altars, in which the deities are enshrined.

Large, famous shrines, such as Meiji Shrine in Tokyo, attract visitors from all over the country. At these shrines, religious artifacts, good-luck charms, and ornaments are sold (technically they are actually exchanged for donations) at booths or other buildings on the grounds.

Visiting shrines and temples in present-day Japan is often more of a weekend recreational outing than a religious observance, but visits are customary on special occasions such as births, birthdays, and New Year's. Virtually all shrines and temples in the country sponsor at least one festival during the course of a year.

Also popular are Shinto rituals for ground-breaking events and celebrations marking the completion of the frame-work of new buildings.

28

Inns as Portals to Japan's Past

Japan's *ryokan* (rio-kahn), or inns, appeared in great numbers in the mid-1600s and have flourished ever since. In many ways, they are like time portals to the country's past. By perpetuating the traditional culture that grew out of court life in Kyoto from AD 794 to 1868, Japan's inns have made it possible for people today to enjoy some of the highly refined experiences that were perfected over the centuries by the clan lords and members of the imperial family.

In these inns, one finds the epitome of Japanese aesthetics—the pliant reed-mat floors, the beautiful sliding door panels, the *tokonoma* altars, the exquisite tableware produced by master artisans, the sensual yukata robes, the stimulating hot baths, the traditional foods, and the kind and quality of service honed for centuries to elevate every guest to the level of royalty.

Popular inns, particularly those outside of the major cities, are invariably located in areas of scenic beauty, often overlooking the sea, a river or lake, or a stunning, stream-carved gorge. Many sites are further enhanced by the subtle, natural beauty of Japanese landscaping.

It is also in Japan's traditional inns that the visitor can see and experience Japanese etiquette in its purest form.

Upon entering the *genkan* (gane-kahn), or foyer, of an inn you will be welcomed by kimono-clad maids. Remove your shoes in the foyer, step up to the inn floor, and don slippers to be worn in the hallway and public areas. After being guided to your room, which is typically oriented to take the fullest possible advantage of the scenic view, you are directed to exchange your street clothes for yukata and provided with tea and a snack, usually fruit or tiny cubes of bean jam.

This begins a totally Japanese experience that will allow you to employ many of the rules of etiquette discussed throughout this book, from sitting and eating on the floor to bathing.

All meals and drinks are served in your room, unless you are with a group that is served communal meals in a large dining hall. When you want service you use an interphone or push a call button. Toilets are usually located outside of the rooms; at many inns the commodes will be elongated ceramic bowls, at floor level, that flush.

Keep in mind that the hallway and public area slippers are never worn into rooms with *tatami* (tah-tah-me) reed-mat floors or in the bathrooms. Instead, leave your hallway slippers outside the bathroom door and don the special slippers that are provided for bathroom use. When you see slippers outside of a bathroom, you know it is occupied.

Your yukata may also be worn outside of the inn, whether for a walk, a shopping excursion, or even playing golf. There are, of course, a right way and a wrong way to wear the yukata. Its left side should be wrapped over its right side. Right-over-left wrapping is reserved for the dead. Men wrap the yukata sash or belt low around their hips and tie it on the right side. Women wrap the sash around their waists and tie it in the back.

If it is rainy, the inn will provide you with an umbrella, often a traditionally styled one made of colorful paper. Make a note to find out if your inn has a *mongen* (moan-gane) or "closing time" when the front door is locked. If it does and you plan to be out after that time, make sure you know where the entry doorbell is located.

Visitors who choose to stay in traditional Japanese inns should be aware that rates are based on rooms that typically accommodate five people, with the charge per person prorated on that basis. If there are only three guests occupying the room the per person charge goes up so that the total revenue for the room is the same as when it is fully occupied. Some *ryokan* owners are advocating that this practice be changed to the system used by Western hotels to avoid confusing tourists, so it is advisable for visitors to inquire about the rate system prior to confirming reservations. Inn rates generally include two meals a day.

29

The Art of Arts & Crafts

Japan's international renown as a trendsetter in the design world is well deserved. Western visitors to Japan often find themselves returning home with many times the baggage they arrived with.

Those who spend even a few days in the country are invariably touched by the special, uniquely Japanese aesthetic they see everywhere around them—in architecture, interior design, fashion, and the amazing technological gadgetry that has been a hallmark of Japanese culture in the West for more than half a century.

The Western appreciation for things Japanese is nothing new. When the first Westerners of record stumbled onto Japan in the early 1540s, the discovery of the islands soon resulted in an influx of foreign traders and Christian missionaries. Among the many things that astounded these first European visitors to Japan was the incredible craftsmanship of its handicrafts and arts. They found the aesthetic appeal and the quality of Japanese-produced goods both seductive and fascinating.

This tradition of artistic excellence finds its roots in Shinto, which holds that all materials have spirits and beauty of their own and that it is up to craftspeople to bring them out.

Shinto takes a holistic view of the size and shape of things, how they are to be used, and their relationship with people. In the creation of traditional Japanese goods, the essence and spirit of the materials used were both respected and revered, resulting in harmony of shape, size, feel, and composition.

After generations of refining their designs and techniques, Japan's master artists and craftspeople achieved a kind and quality of beauty that transcended the obvious surface manifestations of their materials—beauty that is described as *yugen* (yuu-gane), meaning "mystery" or "subtlety." It radiates a kind of spiritual essence.

Yugen is a word I recommend Westerners learn and use while in Japan because it clearly identifies a concept that in other languages requires several sentences to explain—and in itself is an example of the traditional Japanese propensity to refine things down to their essence, dispensing with the superfluous.

By the tenth century, *yugen* sense had become so deeply embedded in Japanese culture that it was no longer merely a religious or artistic aesthetic—it was reflected in everything the Japanese did, from designing and building castles, gardens, homes, and palaces to the creation of hand-made paper.

The Shinto concepts of harmony, sensuality, and spirituality are cultural factors that remain very much in evidence and in force among Japanese artists and craftspeople in present-day Japan.

Another important factor that distinguishes Japan's traditional arts and crafts, as well as many of its modern products, is the influence of its neighbors. Beginning around AD 300, Chinese ideas and products began trickling into Japan, mostly through Korea and via Korean immigrants to the islands. The ancient Chinese custom of a master-apprentice approach to the arts and crafts was one of the most important artistic philosophies that Japan adopted during this period.

But the Japanese didn't just imitate the Chinese and Koreans. They institutionalized and ritualized the master-apprentice training methods, adding to them the concept of *kaizen* (kigh-zen), or continuous improvement. Within a few generations these methods had been totally Japanized and their quality raised to the level of fine art. (Japan's reputation for producing cheap imitations of Western products from around 1890 on was not of Japan's own making. Foreign importers who flocked to Japan to take advantage of both the extraordinary skill to be found there and the low wages were the ones who determined the quality of Japanese exports until around 1960. At that time the Japanese were able to gain control of both their manufacturing and export industries and begin producing products superior to most of the ones produced in the West.)

The influence of the Japanese aesthetic on Westerners varies from very weak to very strong, but it influences everyone to some degree. To the sensitive person, it has a calming, soothing effect on the intellect and the spirit, and creates a harmonious repose with nature.

30

People-Watching

People visiting Japan shortchange themselves if they limit their sightseeing to its historical grandeurs and modern-day high-rise buildings, "bullet trains," and shops that make Los Angeles' Rodeo Drive look dowdy.

One of the keys to getting a real feel for Japan, and thereby getting the most out of your visit there, is to rub elbows with Japanese people by going to crowded dining, entertainment, and shopping areas and simply "people-watching"—appreciating the way regular people go about living their everyday lives as the crowd goes to and fro.

There are literally thousands of outstanding locations for people-watching in Tokyo alone, but to make things easier for visitors the following paragraphs outline several specific spots worth visiting, each of which has a personality of its own.

Three of these locations are within a short walk of each other. They are the main Ginza intersection where Hibiya-Harumi and Chuo streets intersect at Ginza 4-chome; the Sukiyabashi intersection, where Hibiya Street intersects with Sotobori Street about 200 yards west of the Ginza intersection; and the Hibiya theater and restaurant district another 200 yards or so to the west.

Since the late 1800s, most Tokyo residents have considered the Ginza 4-chome intersection to be the unofficial center of the city. Its famous Mitsukoshi and Wako department stores are historical icons. (Really old-timers may recall that the Mitsukoshi department store building on the northeast corner of the intersection was the main post exchange for the U.S. military during the 1945–1952 occupation of Japan. They also might remember that there was a U.S.-run cafeteria that served hamburgers and milk shakes in the basement of the Wako department store building on the northwestern corner of the intersection.)

The nearby Hibiya restaurant and shopping district is the location of the Tokyo branch of the famous Takarazuka Theater, which features all-female revues on the scale seen in Paris and Las Vegas—complete with women donning false mustaches to play male roles. Hundreds of young girls regularly flock to the stage entrance to see their favorite stars come and go, and they themselves become an attraction.

The Roppongi district is a few minutes on the subway away from the Ginza and Hibiya areas, and it is a people-watching place with its own peculiar image. It consists of a maze of narrow streets that are home to hundreds of bars, nightclubs, and restaurants that run the gamut from dives to posh establishments where only the best is on offer. The district is a major draw for foreign residents, film stars, fashion models, and others wanting to make some kind of statement.

Shibuya, a few minutes further in a southwesterly direction (on the Yamanote commuter train loop line that encircles central Tokyo, as well as the terminus of the Ginza subway line), is a nighttime and weekend mecca for young people who are drawn to the area by its plethora of clothing and accessory shops, restaurants, bars, bookstores, record stores, and the like. The statue of Hachiko (hah-chee-koh—

the name of a faithful dog.) in front of Shibuya station is the place to meet friends and see and be seen.

Wide, tree-lined Omotesando Boulevard (which begins in front of Harajuku station, one station northwest of Shibuya) now competes with Chuo Avenue (the main Ginza thoroughfare) as the city's most popular strolling street.

In addition to the upscale fashion shops and restaurants fronting on Omotesando, the district's maze of side streets are chock full of shops carrying the kind of clothing favored by the far-out young. In fact, it is the dress, make-up, and behavior of the thousands of young people who flock to Harajuku on holidays and weekends that attracts hordes of sightseers.

Shinjuku, accessible from the second station after Harajuku on the Yamanote line as well as from several other subway lines, is another of Tokyo's huge city-sized districts that are microcosms of an astounding concentration of dining, entertainment, and shopping facilities that make the country a paradise for residents and visitors alike.

One could easily visit such well-known locations as Akasaka, Aoyama, Asakusa, and go on down the alphabetical line. All of these places have their own special appeal, but the few noted should be enough to introduce visitors to the remarkable flavor of life in Japan.

31

Japan's Greening

Visitors to Tokyo should be aware that in addition to being one of the world's most extraordinary cities in terms of facilities and amenities—including more restaurants, bars, clubs, department stores, business centers, subways, and commuter trains than any other city on the planet—Tokyo is also a world-leader in adding green elements to its city scape.

Like many American cities, by the turn of the twenty-first century Tokyo had undertaken a massive program to turn its huge urban area into an oasis of rooftop and open-field gardens. This ambitious plan was well underway within this century's first decade.

But the urban gardens of Tokyo are not just for show. Together they include virtually all of the popular edible vegetables, as well as rice, which is still a major staple of the diet of most older Japanese and a symbol of the country's culinary tradition.

The city-wide program was designed to dramatically increase the amount of natural space within its environs, including forests, rivers, rice paddies, and gardens on the rooftops of office buildings. Tokyo's Metropolitan Government took the lead in promoting this greening campaign by constructing a

770-square meter (900-square yard) garden on the rooftop of its high-rise headquarters on the west side of town.

A city ordinance requires that all new, expanded, or improved buildings with 3,000 square meters (3,500 square yards) of space or more must cover at least 20 percent of their land and rooftops with plants, trees, or other greenery.

The famed Isetan department store in Shinjuku replaced the amusement rides that had been on its rooftop with a garden—which now not only attracts more visitors than the amusement center, but also brought summertime rooftop temperatures down by 18 degrees. School children and young women planted a rice paddy on top of one of the signature Mori building towers in Roppongi, known around the world as one of the city's prime entertainment districts.

Another feature of this phenomenon was the founding of membership gardens in open areas of the outlying wards. These gardens include clubhouses where members can change into their work clothes, shower, eat, drink, exchange information, and socialize.

One of the largest of these communal gardens is located in Seijo, an upscale residential area in Setagaya Ward just fifteen minutes from the core of Tokyo. The 500-square meter (600-square yard) walled-in area, called Agris Seijo, is divided into 300 plots to accommodate members who pay annual fees for the privilege of having their own urban gardens.

Suburban cities like Musashino also got into the act with garden centers on city property that feature a variety of seasonal agricultural events that residents may attend free of charge.

As greening grew popular, Pasona, Inc., a well-known temporary staffing company, inaugurated a training program for people who wanted to get an Agri-MBA. Classes are given three times a week at the company's headquarters in Otemachi, one of Tokyo's premiere business centers. The course includes a seven-day training session on a working farm. Some of the students say they are taking the course to get out of the business rat-race and make their living by farming.

This new phenomenon, originally known as "hobby farming," quickly began spreading throughout Japan with many new agricultural entrepreneurs becoming professional, full-time farmers. This augurs well for the growing number of people worldwide who are yearning for a saner, simpler life.

An unintended benefit of the greening of Japan has been the additional ambiance it has created for foreign tourists. When this is added to the extraordinary integration of Japan's mass transportation systems and its dining, shopping, recreation, and sightseeing facilities, it makes Japan one of the most attractive and convenient travel destinations in the world.

32

Business in Japan

There are several characteristics that distinguish Japanese companies and often create problems for foreign businesspeople. These characteristics include a degree of formality that sets them apart from American companies; a hierarchical structure that is similar to what exists in military organizations; a reliance on management by consensus rather than the initiative of individuals; strict forms of behavior that eschew most of the light-hearted casual joking and horseplay that is common in many foreign companies; and extraordinary employee loyalty.

All of these things provide Japanese companies with a team mentality that often gives them special advantages when they deal with foreign companies. But these very qualities may also handicap them in their dealings with international companies where individuals have authority to make fast, major decisions.

One of the best pieces of advice that foreign businesspeople can take to heart in their dealings with Japanese companies is to treat them like small countries that are, in fact, democratic—meaning that many people in the typical company have a say in what it does and how it does it.

It therefore follows that Japanese companies should be approached with many of the trappings of diplomatic protocol, including detailed preparations and extensive meetings with several lower and middle levels of management before top executives are brought in.

The initial approach as well as on-going communications and meetings invariably involve a substantial degree of *nemawashi* (nay-mah-wah-she), literally "root revolving," but figuratively meaning "informal behind-the-scenes conversations and lobbying."

This said, there are a growing number of well-known Japanese companies with presidents who take more individual initiative in management—at least as far as public pronouncements are concerned. Given the powerful role that traditional culture continues to play in Japanese behavior, this public image of "Lone Ranger" presidents in Japan should be taken with the proverbial grain of salt. However, there are exceptions to this cautionary word—namely companies that are run by their founders, particularly those in high-tech fields such as Internet enterprises.

One special point to keep in mind is that the Japanese do not view contracts as agreements and protocol that are set in stone. They see them as an agreement to engage in business and to continually adjust the relationship to conform to changing circumstances. This means that after signing a contract with a Japanese company it is imperative for the foreign side to stay in close touch with all of the levels of management on the Japanese side in order to keep the relationship on an even keel.

Also important is that the Japanese generally do not engage in detailed or hard-nosed negotiating at the meeting table. This is nearly impossible because there is usually no single individual in a section, division, or company who can speak for everyone else. Instead, much of the wheeling and dealing takes place outside of the conference room, often in the evening at dinners or drinking parties where formal "daytime etiquette" can be dispensed with and individuals can say what they really think—and what they really want.

A deeply embedded trait of Japanese businesspeople that often surprises Westerners is a distrust of people who base all their comments and reactions on strictly logical thinking. In the Japanese mindset, *rikutsu-poi* (ree-kute-sue-poy) or "being overly logical" is negative rather than positive.

This doesn't mean that the Japanese can't or don't think and act logically, but at the beginning of relationships they generally camouflage such behavior in terms relating to the personal, human side of business. In fact, the Japanese are often more logical and thorough in their preparations and the results they achieve than many Westerners. The Japanese take more time and make use of "fuzzy" or circular thinking, which results in a holistic approach.

Since the 1980s it has been the official policy in Japan to follow a holistic approach to business, expressed in the term *yūgō-ka* (yuu-goh-kah), or "the fusion of ideas and technology"—something the Japanese generally do exceptionally well.

The sections that follow include other business-related points that play key roles in doing business in Japan.

33

Introductions & Relationships

Establishing a relationship with a Japanese company can be a long, drawn-out affair because a number of cultural imperatives must be satisfied in the process.

The first of these is the orchestration of a proper introduction. Self-introductions, although common in the United States and other Western countries, were traditionally unacceptable in Japan. They went against important culture values by requiring an individual to be aggressive, which was considered impolite, and gave the other party no way of quickly verifying identities or claims. There was no mutually known third party who could take responsibility for the new acquaintance in case anything went wrong—a *hoshōnin* (hoh-shohh-neen), or guarantor.

In addition, people were always reluctant to take on new obligations or relationships, which would increase their responsibilities and the possibility of encountering problems. This worry grew from a long-standing social tradition: In the past, the Japanese limited their close ties to members of their own groups. This led to accepting new people into the outer fringes of their circles only if the newcomers came to them with introductions from known and trusted contacts.

By the same token, it was a significant advantage to have a *shokaij* (show-kie-johh), or introduction, from a someone the other party was obligated to—a close relative, a business associate, or a person of high rank.

This Japanese attitude toward self-introductions, especially by foreign company representatives, started diminishing in the 1960s when the country began "going international," but it is still an important factor in establishing business contacts. Even today, the chances of being received with something other than polite ceremony and subtle rejection are greatly enhanced if you start off with an introduction from an individual or company the other party knows and respects.

Even with an impressive introduction, the structure of Japanese society and the formalities demanded by its etiquette make it difficult for the Japanese to quickly establish a working relationship with a new contact. The Japanese themselves must be able and willing to spend a considerable amount of time nurturing a new relationship with personal visits, by eating and drinking together, and gradually establishing the credibility and confidence necessary to be taken seriously.

Broadly speaking, this is also true for foreign businesspeople attempting to create and nurture relationships with individuals in Japanese companies. Depending on their company, rank, and what they want, however, foreigners are often given the benefit of the doubt and the process of developing a meaningful relationship may proceed faster.

A factor that sometimes misleads foreign businesspeople is the generous amount of money normally allotted for Japanese managers to spend on clients and potential business contacts. Many foreigners delude themselves into thinking they have made a great impression after they have been given the royal treatment by free-spending Japanese contacts.

In any event, it is wise to keep Japanese etiquette and the special sensitivities of the Japanese in mind when embarking on any business relationship there. It is also important to remember that the ability of the Japanese to speak English is not always an accurate reflection of their degree of Westernization or comfort level with Western behavior. This is especially true of those who have studied English only in Japan.

34

Name Cards &
How to Exchange Them

Name cards are especially important in Japan, not only in business but in all professional and official situations. Even people who aren't directly involved with the business world usually have their own name cards.

The importance of these cards derives from feudal Japan's vertically arranged social structure. The prescribed etiquette for every individual was primarily determined by his or her clan, class, group affiliation, or position. Following the correct etiquette was critical; in some cases one's life depended on it. This made it imperative for people meeting for the first time to quickly and accurately identify each other's position in the social hierarchy in order to determine which rules of etiquette applied. If no relationship was desired, strangers ignored each other—at a safe distance when possible, and with studied indifference when close contact was unavoidable. When a relationship was desired or unavoidable, a mode of introduction that was appropriate to the stranger's rank and class was established.

In the past, introductions among ranking, high-class people were very formal and stylized. Warriors preparing for combat to the death would often go through an elaborate ritual of self-introduction that would not have been out of place on a Shakespearean stage. In a parody of the upper classes and sword-carrying samurai, professional gamblers also devised lengthy, intricate ways of introducing themselves to rivals—and sometimes to the law.

Prior to the Meiji Restoration in 1868, class, rank, and group identity could often be determined by visible factors, including clothing and family crests. Each class and many occupations had distinctive uniforms, some of which were prescribed by law. The style of a man's kimono could indicate his rank; the style of a woman's kimono indicated her marital status and age.

With the abolition of the feudal system, these visible signs were less frequently displayed, and some, such as sword-carrying by the samurai class, disappeared altogether. As Japan modernized, large commercial conglomerates such as Mitsui, Mitsubishi, and Sumitomo began to replace clans as the primary affiliation of a significant percentage of the population (in its pre-World War II heyday, Mitsui had three million employees.)

This system resulted in the appearance of many new ranks that covered a broader spectrum of people and made it impossible for individuals to identify others by visible signs—although company lapel buttons came to replace the old feudal clan crests. While identifying one another was no longer a life-or-death issue, it remained of vital importance because it related directly to one's social and business standing. If businesspeople and professionals were unable to quickly establish the company or group affiliation and ranking of those around them, etiquette restraints would make it virtually impossible for them to communicate properly. The name card came to serve this vital function.

The regular use of name cards was apparently begun centuries ago in China by an imperial court eunuch who rose to the position of minister of the empire. (He favored very large, pink cards.) Name cards did not become common in Japan, however, until the 1870s, following the downfall of the last shogunate, the abolition of the samurai and clan systems, and the beginning of industrialization on a massive scale.

Despite the changes in the national government and the abolition of the feudalistic clans, more than two thousand years of cultural conditioning could not be swept away overnight—or even in several generations. Class, rank, and seniority consciousness remained the paramount force controlling interpersonal relationships in Japanese society. This fundamental factor was to propel name cards into a vital role in everyday Japanese life.

In keeping with the Japanese penchant for carefully structured behavior, the manner of exchanging name cards, called *meishi kokan* (may-she koe-kahn), is still fairly ritualized. And, as may be expected, it requires a certain amount of know-how and experience to properly exchange name cards in the Japanese way.

The first step that foreign businesspeople should take when planning a trip to Japan is to have their names and titles translated into the Romanized Japanese syllables outlined at the beginning of this book and printed on the reverse side of their cards. This is very important because native speakers of Japanese usually can't pronounce foreign names just from their English spellings. For example, *Greenberg* becomes *Guriinbagu* (Guu-reen-baah-guu), and *Carter* becomes *Kātā* (Kah-tah). It is very important that the Japanese language side is up when you present your name card.

The highest form of *meishi kokan* etiquette calls for you to directly face the individual you're about to give your card to, and hold your card in both hands with the Japanese side up and facing the recipient. As you receive the other person's card, say your name along with one of the usual greetings such as: "My name is Smith. I'm pleased to meet you." (Note that although the word *san* is analogous to "Mr." in English, you should never add it to your own name.) Or, if you want to say it in Japanese: *Smith desu. Hajimemashite, dōzo yoroshiku* (Suu-me-suu dess. Hah-jee-may-mahsh-tay, doe-zoe yoe-roshe-kuu).

As soon as you receive the other person's card you should look at the name and title on it, determine the degree of respect due him or her, and then bow accordingly. If the person you have just met is significantly senior to you and you want to make a good impression, your bow should be at least a little more than a slight tilting of the head. A conspicuously deep bow is not called for, however. If you are senior and there is no reason for you to cater to the individual you are meeting, your bow can be shallower and shorter.

The procedure for exchanging cards is the same for each individual in the group. Keep in mind that the exchange should not be hurried. If you are seated and introduce yourself to several people, it is impolite to deal your cards as if you were playing poker. Instead, carefully hand a card to each of your counterparts, even if you have to stretch or get up to do it. Of course, there will be occasions when you are across a table or in some other awkward situation that doesn't allow this. You can still smile and bow your head slightly to each individual that you pass your card to.

It is also good etiquette to keep your name cards in a plastic or leather holder. This not only keeps them together but also helps prevent them from becoming smudged and worn. It is impolite to hand out a less-than-pristine card.

Another point: the more Westernized the Japanese are, the less you need to be concerned about ritual, especially bowing and using both hands to hold your card when presenting it. A growing number of Japanese do not bow or follow traditional etiquette when meeting or exchanging name cards with foreigners.

The behavior of the Japanese you meet will quickly make obvious the level of etiquette that is appropriate for you to follow when with them.

35

Vague Language

In formal business and political situations, Japanese are noted for not saying precisely what they really think up front. Instead, the custom is to express themselves in subtle or oblique terms, only gradually revealing their real position and intentions. This is such an ingrained cultural trait that it has influenced both the structure and the use of the Japanese language.

The result is that the Japanese seldom if ever respond to proposals and ideas with explicit *yes* or *no* answers. Saying something would be difficult, for example, generally means no. Using the common expression *kentō shimasu* (ken-tohh she-mahss), or "I/we will study it," also often means that no action will be taken.

The famous terms *tatemae* (tah-tay-my) and *honne* (hone-nay) are the "cultural umbrellas" that explain the characteristic approach of the Japanese in business negotiations. *Tatemae* refers to a facade or a front, which is what the Japanese typically put forward first. *Honne* refers to the real thing, real desires and intentions that are revealed only gradually as the talks proceed.

This behavior is, of course, part of the overall etiquette in which creating friction or irritation is considered taboo and the need for surface harmony takes precedence over other considerations.

There are now many Japanese whose exposure to Western concepts and behavior has influenced them to the point that they will speak directly and make specific commitments. But generally speaking they are able to do this only when acting privately on matters that concern them alone. In business situations where others are concerned, the Japanese are still compelled to go by the rules of the group, which dictate that decisions must be based on a broad consensus of lower, middle, and upper management.

Some Japanese brain specialists claim that the way Japanese and Westerners think and behave is different because we do not use the left and right sides of our brains in the same way. They maintain that Japanese thinking is primarily based on cultural intuition and the need for harmony, which are right-brain functions, while Western thinking emphasizes intellect and logic, which are left-brain functions. True or not, the group orientation of Japanese society makes it virtually impossible for individuals to make unilateral statements or commitments for themselves or their groups, except when one is chosen to act as spokesman for the group after consensus has been reached and a decision formalized.

Before consensus is reached, nobody in a Japanese company or organization really knows what the outcome of any discussion or negotiation will be. The more they are pressed for a response, the more vague and unresponsive they are likely to be. Pressure beyond a certain point can result in a complete breakdown in communication.

Japanese obfuscation is usually not designed to maliciously mislead, delay, or cause problems. It is designed to maintain harmony while allowing the group approach to work.

There are specific rules of etiquette for dealing with this obfuscation factor: avoid direct confrontation, don't put anyone on the spot, and use third parties—insiders if possible—to give regular readings on the status of any ongoing negotiations or project planning. Sometimes these readings are accurate and helpful; at other times they may not be. There is always an element of uncertainty.

If you have a close, personal relationship with an upper-level member of the Japanese group, someone who is at the section-chief level or above, take him or her out for a drinking session. In this informal environment, you can often get a fairly good idea about whether your project is proceeding smoothly. The casual atmosphere will generally enable this colleague to level with you.

If you find yourself in a situation in which the intent or desire of an individual or company is unclear and you really need to know where you stand, your best recourse is to ask a trusted mutual friend or neutral go-between to make discreet inquiries on your behalf.

36

Criticism Taboos

Japanese can be much more sensitive to criticism than they are to compliments. This sensitivity to criticism arose from the importance of correct behavior in traditional culture. An essential part of proper behavior was to avoid being shamed and shaming others as a result of behaving in an unacceptable manner.

One of the best-known anecdotes dating from Japan's mythological age involves a god who shamed his fellow gods and goddesses by his failure to follow prescribed etiquette. He was banned from the heavens.

Being shamed by a personal failure or by an implied failure has traditionally been the worst fate that could befall a Japanese. There was an equally powerful feeling that the only way the shame could be expiated was through revenge. If circumstances were such that revenge was impossible and the matter was important, suicide was often the only acceptable alternative.

In fact, suicide among Japan's samurai class was such a common method of expiating the "sin" of violating etiquette during the Tokugawa period that the government enacted numerous edicts prohibiting such behavior.

Japanese history and contemporary Japanese literature and movies are filled with acts of revenge or suicide, brought on by someone having been shamed, either because of his or her own behavior or through the criticism of others.

Even in modern Japan, hardly a year goes by that several ranking executives do not take their own lives as a result of being shamed by some failure or criticism. Young people, criticized by parents or teachers, are also prone to commit suicide.

While criticism by foreigners is not likely to bring on suicide, visiting and resident foreigners should nevertheless be careful about criticizing anyone to their face, whether they are employees, hotel clerks, taxi drivers, or strangers.

Even when the criticism is fully and obviously deserved, the shame it produces may have unpleasant repercussions. If you have something to get off your chest, it is better to report it to the supervisor or employing organization of the person you wish to criticize.

Foreign residents of Japan, particularly businesspeople who work with Japanese people on a daily basis, should be especially cautious when handling situations where criticism is warranted. One of the best ways to convey criticism is to use a third party, preferably someone who is older or higher-ranking than the person being criticized and has had considerable experience handling such sensitive matters.

Another approach, without a third party, is to begin the session with praise and compliments and then bring up the bad news indirectly, stressing the positive results you want to achieve without specifically criticizing the person with whom you are speaking. Being especially sensitive to such things, the Japanese concerned will clearly understand that he or she is being criticized, but will not be put in the position of losing face.

Interestingly, Japanese managers themselves criticize staff members openly in front of their co-workers. The reason for this is that the staff in each section functions as a team, with little difference in duties and obligations and, consequently, treatment by superiors. Disciplining a member openly reinforces the idea that the whole group is responsible for the behavior of its members. This approach is not advisable for foreign managers in Japan, since such an action would likely be seen in a negative light.

A favorite technique used by Japanese managers is to invite the person targeted for criticism out drinking after work. After both have drunk enough to forgo normal dictates of etiquette, the manager can frankly say what has been on his or her mind all along, but, again, in such a way to allow the other party to avoid losing face.

Many managers who use the after-hours drinking technique specialize in using humor to remove some of the sting while making their point. It is not necessary for them to be too explicit. Japanese are so attuned to the tenor of such situations that their "cultural telepathy" allows them to get the message loud and clear.

Another point that should be mentioned is that many foreigners, particularly Americans, are chronic complainers about their own country's perceived failings and constantly make critical comments to the Japanese. Rather than endearing the complainers to the Japanese, this kind of behavior is regarded as a cheap attempt to flatter them and drastically lowers the foreigner's image.

The Japanese can be vociferously critical of their politicians on every level of government, but this does not diminish their pride in Japan. They regard misbehavior by politicians as a serious blot on Japan's image and accuse offenders of shaming the country and the people at large.

37

The Pitfalls of
Praise in Japan

In a society in which adhering strictly to a formalized etiquette was equated with both character and morality,
and where lapses in etiquette were traditionally dealt with
harshly, it is interesting to note that childhood training in
Japanese etiquette was affected more through praise and
example than by threat of punishment.

During infancy and childhood, Japanese were effusively
praised when they acted appropriately—whether it was bowing correctly, using chopsticks properly, or singing a song
well. Once they approached the teen years, however, they
were expected to know and abide by proper etiquette and
such compliments become rare—the idea being that performing the proper act in the correct manner at the appropriate time was simply expected, and did not warrant special praise.

However, the Japanese are still inclined to be overly effu-
sive in their praise of foreign visitors who show an understanding of or skill related to Japanese culture, such as the
ability to use chopsticks or speak some Japanese.

In earlier times the Japanese generally believed that
their language was so different and so difficult to learn that

foreigners could not learn it. However, during the early years of the Tokugawa Shogunate the government decided not to take any chances. It issued a decree making it a capital offense for a Japanese to teach Japanese to a foreigner— a security measure that was to have extraordinary ramifications over the next several generations.

As late as the 1950s, a foreigner who was able to speak very good Japanese would frequently encounter people who were so conditioned to believe that foreigners could not speak their language that they actually did not understand when addressed in Japanese. One typically had to say in Japanese something like "Hey! I just spoke to you in Japanese!" to break through this mental barrier.

The group orientation of Japanese society still generally precludes singling out individuals for special recognition. Outstanding athletes on sports teams, for example, have to demonstrate an almost ridiculous degree of modesty regarding their skill and accomplishments in order to prevent their teammates from ostracizing them and the public from regarding them as arrogant.

Company and university employees who innovate or invent something that is quite remarkable are often virtually ignored by their coworkers, who consider that any special recognition of the individual would reflect badly on them. There have been numerous cases in recent years where Japanese inventors were not recognized in Japan until they had become famous abroad and were widely lauded by their foreign colleagues and the international news media.

Some Japanese employees who made breakthrough inventions have gone to the un-Japanese-like extreme of suing their employers in order to get some recognition for their accomplishments. This has resulted in a growing public argument that Japanese society should recognize the efforts of individuals in order to encourage personal initiative. But old cultural programming dies hard, and the praise of individuals still arouses rancor in many academic and professional circles.

When foreign visitors, unaware of this code, compliment individual Japanese, it may embarrass those receiving the praise and sometimes result in their colleagues becoming envious to the point of never again accepting them as full, trusted members of the group.

Company managers have to be very diplomatic in the way they treat superior employees. Direct public compliments to Japanese professionals by foreigners can have the opposite effect of what is intended. Japanese managers go to great lengths to create and intensify the team concept. When an individual member of the team accomplishes something extraordinary, the idea is that the group as a whole gets the credit.

This level of sensitivity and group-orientation has diminished significantly in present-day Japan, especially in the international business community and among the younger generations. They may respond in a modest manner but they appreciate compliments and praise as much as anyone else.

This said, the cultural antenna of the Japanese is especially sensitive to a lack of *makoto* (mah-koe-toe), or sincerity, in voice and manner, and to what in early times was known as *gomasuri* (go-mah-suu-ree), literally "grinding sesame seeds," a word that in modern parlance refers to flattery. The real word for flattery is *oseji* (oh-say-jee).

The Japanese themselves are masters at flattering people, particularly foreign visitors and newly arrived businesspeople. They learned a long time ago that most Westerners are especially susceptible to such treatment and can often be disarmed and manipulated by the copious application of *oseji.*

38

Sayonara—"If it must be so!"

Many people are familiar with the Japanese expression *sayonara* (sah-yoh-nah-rah), or "good-bye." But few are aware that the literal meaning of the term is "if it must be so"—a very lyrical and emotional way of expressing the sense of loss and sadness often felt when parting.

Unfortunately, the Japanese habit of incorporating foreign words into their language has significantly reduced the use of *sayonara*, especially among young people who prefer the English "bye-bye." Young school girls, in particular, engage in a prolonged ritual of waving and saying "bye-bye" to each other when they part for the day, continuing until their friends are out of sight.

But *sayonara* is not the only Japanese way to say good-bye. There are a number of set Japanese expressions specifically used when leaving and returning home that can easily be added to the vocabulary of foreign visitors. These include:

Itte kimasu (eat-tay kee-mahss), which is more or less the Japanese equivalent of "I'll be back." This is commonly said when leaving home for work or to go shopping, and it may also be used in a company situation when one is leaving on some kind of errand or to attend a meeting. The literal meaning of this phrase is "I'm going and coming."

Itte irasshai (eat-tay ee-rah-shy) is the automatic response to *itte kimasu*. It is said by the person staying home or in the office. The literal meaning of this phrase is "please go and come," and it functions as "See you later," or perhaps more aptly, "Come back safely."

Tadaima (tah-die-mah) is what one says upon returning home or to the office. It's the equivalent of "I'm home," or "I'm back."

O-kaerinasai (oh-kye-ree-nah-sie) is the ritualized response to *tadaima*. It figuratively means "welcome home" or "welcome back."

Other conventionalized expressions used when bidding someone farewell include:

O-genki de (oh-gane-kee day). This means something like "go in good health," and is said to someone who is leaving for an extended trip. It is commonly used when it is uncertain if and when you will see the people again, or if their health is of concern.

Kiotsukete (kee-oh-t'sue-kay-tay) means "be careful" or "take care" and is said to children, older people, or anyone who might face some kind of danger.

Ganbatte (gahn-baht-tay) roughly translates as "hang in there" or "don't give up." It is often called out to people who are engaged in competition or some difficult task, or to those about to embark on a demanding undertaking. The present tense of the verb *ganbarimasu* (gahn-bah-ree-mahss), "I will try my best," is one of the most frequently used expressions in the Japanese language.

Glossary of Useful Terms

Agari (ah-gah-ree). This is the proper term to use when asking for green tea in a sushi shop. In other restaurants and in homes you may ask for an *o'kawari* (oh-kah-wah-ree), which means a refill. The full phrase is *O'Kawari kudasai* (Oh-kah-wah-ree kuu-dah-sie), or literally, "a refill, please."

Baishaku (by-shah-kuu). Proper etiquette in preparing for an arranged marriage is to engage the services of a *baishaku*, or "go-between," who may be a relative, friend, or a professional. *Baishaku* is the formal term for this sort of go-between, but the more common term is *nakodo* (nah-koh-doe). These words mean the same thing, but *baishaku* refers more specifically to marriage go-betweens, while *nakodo* can also be used in business arrangements. A marriage arranged by a go-between is called a *baishaku kekkon* (by-shah-kuu keck-kone), or "go-between marriage."

Banzai (bahn-zye). This is a traditional exclamation shouted as an expression of joy or as a rallying cry before some demanding action. It is shouted three times. Each time the arms are raised over the head with the hands outstretched. When

"Banzai!" is the appropriate cheer at gatherings or events, there is usually a leader who cues the group so that they all shout in unison.

Dōmo (doe-moe). This is the "very" and "much" part of "thank you very much." It can also mean "really." It is used colloquially as "thanks" in very informal situations as well as "thank you" in more formal situations. Like *sumimasen* (sue-me-mah-sen), it can be used to express the idea of "excuse me" or "sorry" when relatively light apologies are called for. This is one of the most commonly used words in the Japanese language.

Dōmo arigatō gozaimashita (doe-moe ah-ree-gah-toe go-zye-mahssh-tah). This is the past tense of "thank you very much," and it is used after something has been done for which you should express appreciation. Since this may be only seconds after the event, its use sometimes appears to overlap its present tense form, *dōmo arigatō gozaimasu*.

Gaiatsu (guy-aht-sue). The nature of the Japanese behavioral system is so inclusive and comprehensive it generally prevents individuals and people in specific groups from advocating and initiating changes on their own, as a result of which they typically attempt to enlist the aid of outside forces to help bring about change, or the whole organization itself changes because of outside pressure. In many cases, especially those involving government bureaucracies, the most effective pressure for change is *gaiatsu*, or "foreign pressure," either from competing foreign companies or foreign national governments. The organizational mindset and behavioral patterns that so often frustrate both Japanese and foreigners are almost always those that respond only to relentless foreign pressure, making it important for foreigners to know the term *gaiatsu* and how to use it.

Gochisōsama deshita (go-chee-so-sah-mah desh-tah). This expression is used when one has been treated to drinks and/or food. It is also often said to the waitstaff as one leaves a restaurant or bar. It roughly translates as "thank you very much for the food/drinks, and thank you for the service."

Gokurōsama (go-kuu-roh-sah-mah). *Kurō* (kuu-roe) by itself means "hardship" or "trouble." *Go* is an honorific prefix. This expression is said by managers or superiors to employees, contract workers, or volunteers who have done their duty and more. They say it after a day's work or upon the completion of a task, especially something that was hard to do and took extra time. The Japanese are sensitive about such recognition and use this expression often to acknowledge the labor of their workers.

Itadakimasu (ee-tah-dah-kee-mahss). This very common expression is used just before you begin to eat or drink with someone, particularly if you are a guest. It acknowledges the fact that you are receiving something from the host as his or her guest. In a relatively small, formal setting such as in a private home or at a party, guests often do not start eating or drinking until the host gives a sign—usually by saying *dōzo* (dohh-zoe), which in this case means "please (start, go ahead)." The guests then say *itadakimasu* and start.

Itadakimashita (ee-tah-dah-kee-mahssh-tah). The past tense of the above word, *itadakimashita* is a polite way of saying "I have eaten/drunk it" or "I have already had a helping/drink." The literal meaning is "I have received (it)."

Kanreki (kahn-ray-kee). This is the celebration marking the sixtieth birthday, which in Japan and elsewhere in Asia is considered an important milestone in life. This arises from the fact that the old calendar system was based on a cycle of sixty years. Living to be sixty was an important achievement because it meant you had completed one full cycle of life and figuratively had been reborn as a baby. A popular present on this day was a red sleeveless kimono of the type traditionally worn by babies. It was also popularly held that once men and women reached this age, they could ignore etiquette and responsibility and act like a baby again. In Japan the custom that allowed people to ignore etiquette after they reached sixty applied only to ordinary people in private life.

Today, most people in Japan celebrate their birthdays, with the sixtieth, seventieth, and eightieth birthdays being of special significance.

Nairyo suru (nie-rio sue-rue). This etiquette-related term means "give careful consideration to," and is often used in response to proposals in which there is no real interest. When used, it invariably means that no action will be taken.

O-Jama shimasu (oh-jah-mah she-mahss). *Jama* (jah-mah) means a hindrance, disturbance, or nuisance. When used in this sentence it means "I am going to disturb you." It is said when entering someone's home or office (after being invited in).

O-Jama shimashita (oh-jah-mah she-mahssh-tah). The past tense of *o-jama shimasu*, this phrase is said when leaving someone's home or office after a visit. It means "I have disturbed you."

O-Kaeshi (oh-kye-she). Receiving a gift sometimes makes a return gift, called *o-kaeshi,* mandatory. The return gift does not have to be as elaborate or as expensive as the gift received, particularly if there was a special reason for the person giving the gift and it is quite valuable. The *o-kaeshi* is usually just enough to acknowledge the gift you received and convey your appreciation.

O-Kage-sama de (oh-kah-gay-sah-mah day). In their efforts not to accept responsibility or take credit, the Japanese have developed a number of expressions to share any credit that might be due. The term *o-kage-sama de*, something like "thanks to you," is used to give the other person credit for the speaker's health or success. If you ask someone how they are, a common response is *o-kage-sama de, genki desu* (oh-kah-gay-sah-mah day, gane-kee dess), or "thanks to you, I'm fine."

Okite (oh-kee-tay). This is the Japanese word for commandment, code, law, regulation, or rule, and it is frequently used in reference to the kind of behavior that is expected of members of companies and government bureaucracies. Managers in government offices are noted for the strict way they enforce the prevailing *okite* in their organizations—often by embarrassing, intimidating, and threatening employees with reprisals.

O-Kyaku-san (oh-kyack-sahn). *O-Kyaku-san* (oh-kyack-sahn), or "Honorable guest," is a useful term that allows you to address visitors or guests in a respectful way without knowing their names or social standings. In status-conscious, insult-sensitive Japan, the term gets a considerable amount of use.

O-Machidō-sama deshita (oh-mah-chee-doe-sah-mah desh-tah). This means "I'm sorry I kept you waiting"—a very useful term for foreign visitors and residents to add to their Japanese vocabularies.

O-Saki ni, shitsurei shimasu (oh-sah-kee nee, she-t'sue-ray she-mahss). Proper etiquette calls for those leaving work to first inform or advise their co-workers with the set expression *o-saki ni* (oh-sah-kee nee), meaning, more or less, "I'm going first." *Shitsurei shimasu* means "I'm being rude," so together these mean something like "excuse me for being rude and leaving before you." Leaving without saying anything may be regarded as uncaring. *Shitsurei* itself is also an informal way of saying "excuse me" (for bumping into someone, and so on).

O-Somatsu-sama (oh-soe-maht-sue-sah-mah). This is said by hosts after being thanked by guests for a meal. When guests say *go-chiso sama deshita* (see above) to the host, the host responds with *o-somatsu-sama,* which means more or less "it was nothing elaborate," or in essence "it was nothing special so no thanks are necessary."

O-Tsukare-sama deshita (oh-t'sue-kah-ray-sah-mah desh-tah). The root verb *tsukareru* (t'sue-kah-ray-rue) means "to become tired." It is used in the above form as a combination farewell and an expression of thanks at the close of a long day of hard work. It is a thoughtful and proper thing to say to anyone who works beyond normal hours or works especially hard. It is more polite than *gokurosama*.

San-san-ku-do (sahn-sahn-kuu-doh). This more or less means "three times three equals nine." It refers to the three sips that are taken from three sake cups by the bride and groom as part of the nuptial oath in a Shinto wedding ceremony. Three is regarded as a lucky number in Japan, with three times three resulting in nine, or a "great number," which symbolizes the strength of the wedding vows.

Senbetsu (sen-bate-sue). Custom calls for relatives and friends to give parting gifts, or *senbetsu*, to those leaving on trips, especially when the trips involve lengthy periods abroad. In earlier days, these were actually gift items. Nowadays, however, *senbetsu* almost always refers to a cash gift, and the trip doesn't have to be particularly long. Of course, the traveler is expected to bring something back for the gift giver.

Shitsurei shimasu (she-t'sue-ray she-mahss). The noun *shitsurei* means "a breach of etiquette, a discourtesy." *Shitsurei shimasu* means "I am being [or am about to be] impolite or rude." This can be said when you walk in front of someone, when you are about to leave someone or a group, when you are in the process of slightly disturbing or inconveniencing someone (as when squeezing past in narrow confines), and so on.

Shitsurei shimashita (she-t'sue-ray she-mahssh-tah). The past tense of *shitsurei shimasu*, this is used in the sense of "excuse me" or "pardon me" after you have bumped into someone or otherwise disturbed or inconvenienced them. Such inconveniences include giving out incorrect information or being wrong about something, even if it is relatively unimportant.

Sumimasen (sue-me-mah-sen). Mentioned elsewhere in this text, the original meaning of this expression is "it never ends." It is now used to mean "excuse me" or "pardon me," and also "I'm sorry" and "thank you." It is the most common way of calling out to get the attention of a waiter, waitress, or clerk, and also the most common expression for on-the-spot apologies for seemingly trivial transgressions. Along with *dōmo* (see above) it is one of the most commonly used words in the Japanese language.

Sumimasen deshita (sue-me-mah-sen desh-tah). This is the past tense of *sumimasen;* it is a common apology for something that occurred at an earlier time or date.

Taika naku (tie-kah nah-kuu). Literally this term means "without serious error" and represents one of the key elements in the behavior of the Japanese. Doing anything that upsets the harmony of a Japanese group or organization is serious, resulting in the Japanese being very cautious in following the *taika naku* code in what they say, how they say it and what they do.

Teinei (tay-nay). This is the Japanese word for "polite", "politeness" and "courtesy". A high level of politeness is one of the key, principles of Japanese etiquette, resulting in *teinei* being a commonly used and heard word.

Te-uchi (tay-oo-chee). This is a rhythmic hand-clapping ceremony that is used in Japan to mark the closing of important parties or receptions and the consummation of alliances and business agreements. The hands are usually clapped ten times, in sets of three followed by a single clap. This cycle is then repeated three times.

Yubi-kiri (yuu-bee-kee-ree). The literal translation of *yubi-kiri* is "finger cutting," originally referring to the somewhat gruesome yakuza custom of cutting off the tip of one's little finger to emphasize a promise or to apologize for a serious transgression. Now it also refers to two people hooking their little fingers together and tugging slightly to symbolize a promise they have made. It is common among children and between women in the entertainment trades and their male customers, who make playful promises to each other. Japan's gangsters still adhere to the original meaning of the term, and it is common to see members of this group with the tips of their little fingers missing.

Za-rei (zah-ray). If you want to surprise the Japanese with your knowledge of traditional Japanese etiquette, do the *za-rei*, which means more or less "sitting bow." It is the formal bow made when sitting on a *tatami* reed-mat floor. To accomplish the bow, place the three large fingers of each hand on the floor in front of you and bow forward from the waist. Your little finger and thumb should be joined in a circle. Of course, you should smile broadly when performing this ancient form of etiquette so that everyone will know you are kidding!

Index